Endor ......

For approximately 30 years I have experienced the ministry of Paul and Gloria Johansson. Their pioneering spirit coupled with a passion to see God's people flourish in ministry that engages the culture has motivated me and thousands of others to follow suit. They have been mentors and dear friends to me. This book is another testament to their investing in the next generation. Read it and watch your faith soar to new heights.

REV. DR. DAVID IRELAND
Senior Pastor of Christ Church, Montclair, New Jersey

When Paul and Gloria Johansson came to Nairobi in 1962, we worked very close with them for eight years to establish the All Nations Church and planted many churches in the district. Mary and Gloria ministered to raise up the women's ministry. We have always been as family. The indigenous foundation they built has continued to grow and is stronger today than ever.

REV. SAMUEL & MARY MWATHA
Nairobi, Kenya

Paul and Gloria Johansson are considered to be a true son and daughter of Kenya because their ministry philosophy continues to impact the PEFA Kenya ministry. They taught indigenous principles that helped the church in Nairobi and Central Province to stand firm on their feet. Paul believed in us by handing over the work in Nairobi in 1969 to Pastor Samuel Mwatha. We love you and appreciate your work very much Mzee Paul na Mama Gloria.

BISHOP DR. JOSEPH MOPHAT KILIOBA
President of Pentecostal Evangelistic Fellowship of Africa

Marla and I met Paul and Gloria Johansson at Elim Bible Institute in the early '70s. In 1977 we started planting churches on the southwest Mexican coast. In 1979 Brother Paul dedicated our first church building in Lazaro Cardenas. We will never forget the vision he shared with us of a tsunami wave coming into our city and reaching to Mexico City and returning to the ocean leaving many little pools of water in the mountains. We embraced this word and over the past 40 years have seen God do exactly according to the vision, now with 160 churches in the mountains. They are a spiritual father and mother to us here in Mexico these 40 years. To God be the glory.

REV. DR. JOHN & MARLA SPYKER
Mexico

We are privileged to HONOR Pastor Paul and Gloria Johansson. They graciously embraced us as we joined the ministry of NYSUM 30 years ago. For this, we are eternally grateful to God. Through their courageous faith in pioneering NYSUM, we now train 5,000 urban workers annually. We owe them a great debt for their selfless service and commitment to see urban leaders trained and equipped to reclaim cities for Christ.

REV. PETER & DARLEEN DeARRUDA
New York School of Urban Ministry

"And they came to Elim". . . young, as two. "And they departed from Elim". . . still young, and soon to be one. When the young man offered his bride-to-be "nothing but the will of God," and she agreed, their shared journey of faith and obedience began. Since first knowing Paul and Gloria as consecrated young students at Elim, their story has unfolded as "the will of God" took them afar—to Africa, and then back to Elim again . . . and again, with "NYSUM" in between more than six decades and many "chapters" into their story, they've left their legacy in nations and their mark on generations, and has been woven into many lives and ministries, including mine. Now may it touch your own!

REV. SYLVIA EVANS
Creative Word Ministries

Rev. Paul Johansson is a minister with many gifts but his ability to teach Romans seems to be a special grace given by God. His regular expository lectures through the years at the Brooklyn Tabernacle proved not only a phenomenal blessing to thousands of students but were also instrumental in preparing numerous believers for their future placement in Christian ministry.

REV. JIM CYMBALA
Senior Pastor, The Brooklyn Tabernacle

I owe a great debt of gratitude to Paul and Gloria Johansson for their friendship and support for the 33 years as Joyce and I have been missionaries in China. Together we have witnessed the birth of a movement, from the early days in the '80s when miracles were commonplace, to the explosive growth of the '90s. China has been enriched by seminars and conferences held by Brother Paul and Elim leaders as has been his book, *Free by Divine Decree,* in Mandarin. Over the past 15 years, the movement has become a mighty force, to gather unto the Lamb people from every tribe, race and nation.

REV. KEVIN GRAVES
Founder of Target Ministries, Asia

Mary and I met Paul and Gloria at Elim Bible Institute in 1974 when we arrived to prepare for the mission field. Without any exaggeration, Paul has been one of the most important influences for good in our family and our calling as missionaries. Over the last three decades they have blessed hundreds of Betel leaders and thousands "Betelitos" in our churches and communities around the world. We count him as a true Father of the Church.

REV. ELLIOT TEPPER
Founder and president of Betel Ministry International

Paul and Gloria have been mentors of ours for 45 years. I have traveled with Paul to Canada, Nepal, India and Egypt. Their apostolic/prophetic ministry have impacted not only the world with the power and wisdom of God but have forever blessed my personal and ministerial life. I am forever grateful to Paul and Gloria Johansson.

REV. DR. RON BURGIO
Senior Pastor, Love Joy Church, Buffalo, New York

Paul and Gloria have been our pastors and spiritual parents as they walked with the work in Mexico for about 40 years. They have shaped our families and ministry with their faith and servant hearts. I believe the testimonies in this book, which I've heard for many years, will change and inspire you to believe God for the impossible.

REV. ANDREAS SPYKER
Senior Pastor to Mas Vida Mexico

Paul, you have taught me much about life and, probably more than any other single individual, have shaped my vision of what a real leader should be. You taught me: Love is shown by valuing people above rules; when God gives you a word, forget about yourself and do it; love means being available; encouragement turns dreams into realities; and, although roles change, relationships endure. Thank you, I will not forget your impact on my life.

REV. MICHAEL CAVANAUGH
President, Elim Bible Institute and College, Lima, New York

FAITH ON ASSIGNMENT

The Johansson Journey

Dear Marcela,
may our journey
inspire, greater faith.
Enjoy!
Blessings, Paul & Gloria

Faith on Assignment:
The Johansson Journey of Life and Ministry.
Copyright © 2017 by Paul & Gloria Johansson
with Jodi Hokenson

Library of Congress Control Number: 2017941208
International Standard Book Number:
ISBN-10: 0-692-88298-7
ISBN-13: 978-0-692-88298-6

Published by:
New York School of Urban Ministry
Paul & Gloria Johansson
Bookstore@nysum.org

FIRST EDITION

Cover Photo:
NYC skyline: jon chica parada / istockphoto.com
Kilimanjaro: Byrdyak / istockphoto.com

Printed in the United States of America

Dedication

We lovingly dedicate this book to all those
upon whose shoulders we stand.
Their sacrifices made to establish us in the faith
and to give us a push in the right direction are priceless.
Also, we share this dedication with those who
"come behind us." We pray you will be encouraged
not to give up the vision. You are the best.
You are called to do the "greater things" (Jn. 14:12)
Christ spoke about, and with God's Spirit
all things are possible to those who believe.

*Front cover has placed the New York City skyline
with Mount Kilimanjaro in the background.*

CONTENTS

Introduction

"Kuishi Kwingi ni kuona mengi!" To live long is to see much!
~ Swahili proverb. To write the story of your own life means you
must have a life interesting enough to write about–and what an
interesting life we have lived. As Gloria and I look back at the
goodness of God to allow us the privilege of being part of His
awesome plan to embrace a hurting world, we are humbled.

Being raised in New York City and living near seaports, I
always was intrigued when we stood on the dock and waved
goodbye to missionaries who would be leaving for many years.
Our family and church members stood together singing "God
be with you till we meet again at Jesus' feet." There was something final about that which involved long-term commitment.
These people have always been a rare breed.

There have always been people who have walked to the
beat of a different drum, sometimes out-of-step with the crowds.
To Gloria and me this kind of off-beat walk has been something
not to be ashamed of, but a badge of honor. When we hold the
hand of Someone we trust, we can walk boldly into the unknown
without fear. The conflicts and doubts we faced in our lives only
caused us to hold on tighter to those nail-scarred hands.

The Johansson journey over the past eighty plus years, in
the words of the aforementioned Swahili proverb, still gives us
opportunity to "see much." Position, fame, money, or security
has never been a part of our life decisions. All the things the
world clamors for is passing, but we will not substitute the temporary for the permanent and eternal.

Our two children, Mark and Marcia, have witnessed first-
hand our Christ-centered lifestyle and commitment to what we
believe are the reasons God put us on this earth. They, in turn,
have dedicated their lives to reach out with gentle guidance and

healing hands to fulfill their unique purposes.

Because of God's unlimited grace, He has given us an inheritance on each of the habitable continents. We have taken the message of redemption, to the best of our obedience, to remote places and forgotten people. From a one-stoplight town in Pennsylvania to mega cities of Africa, India, China, Spain, Mexico, and Australia, we have stood on the shoulders of past generations and, more recently, our own parents and grandparents who, though they have passed away, still inspire us today.

Mega thanks to Jodi Hokenson for her diligent effort to listen to our stories and to put them together, piece by piece, into a cohesive whole. Truly we have been surrounded by people who highlight how we are being conformed into the likeness of Jesus.

Elim provided the arena for us to "prove our stuff," but it was only in allowing the Master to work through us for His own purpose that we have had any success at all in loving God and loving people.

SECTION I
PAUL

CHAPTER 1

Our First Voyage

After two-and-a-half years of marriage, my wife Gloria and I packed up all our earthly belongings, boarded the *Robin Gray* freighter at the Brooklyn, New York, port and headed for Mombasa, Kenya. It was March 20, 1959. I had recently celebrated my twenty-third birthday and our son Mark was just seventeen months old. We imagined life in Africa to be different, but as the chilly March winds wrapped around our three bodies that day, we should have known the journey ahead would be filled with more challenges than our limited minds could foresee.

The maximum passenger capacity for the *Robin Gray* was twelve. The day my little family of three set sail the total passenger count was eleven people; however, a heavy load of cargo more than made up for the required tonnage. Gloria and I chose a freighter as our preferred transportation to Kenya mainly because we were allowed 10 cubic feet of cargo in the price of our tickets. This allowed us to take along our son Mark's baby bed and dresser, our bedroom furniture, printing presses for all of the printing we planned to do, and our complete set of newly donated Kitchen Kraft pots and pans.

We first sighted land after twenty-one days at sea. Our world returned to semi-normal as the gyrating sea world stopped shaking and gave way to a beautiful, stable view of Table Top Mountain, Cape Town, South Africa. Despite staying there only one night, it was a very memorable night. After de-boarding the ship, a friendly Englishman approached us and remarked, "It looks like you are strangers." He served as our temporary tour guide by showing us around town and accompanying us on our first dinner experience on the African continent. Because of him—truly an angel sent from God—we felt safe and welcomed into Cape Town.

From there we sailed southeast toward Cape Agulhas and through its monster Cape rollers. Those rogue waves rolled our freighter up and around so intensely I felt like I was caught in the cylinders of a printing press I remembered watching my father run working as a printer at the *Newsday* newspaper on Long Island. Unnerving sound effects accompanied this leg of our journey as it seemed not a loose dish aboard failed to crash when our ship yawed and pitched. I began to question whether or not my little family would survive these killer rollers at sea. In my heart I thanked God for giving my wife the wisdom to take Dramamine while aboard the ship since she suffered from sea sickness, while I did not. Finally, in the midst of the rollers, I rested assured it was God's right hand and His holy arm that would give us His victory—protecting us by His faith to the very end of our journey. Our journey through the dreadful Cape rollers took a very long eighteen hours, but it was the only passage through to our next ports, including Durban, South Africa, along the Indian Ocean.

At last we safely arrived at the Durban port and upon alighting the ship, I contacted the pastor of a local church to ask when the service time was on Sunday morning since we knew we would be at this port for at least the weekend. By the time Sunday rolled around, Gloria and I were ready for some good fellowship and preaching so we headed off to this local church. Instead of allowing me to relax and listen, however, the pastor asked me if I would preach right then and there. Wanting to be ready in every season, I accepted the invitation to preach at that Sunday morning service. The people who attended were so moved by the message of the Gospel, they invited me to continue preaching. Since the freight and not the passengers determined the arrival and departure times of our ship, my first preaching experience on the African continent ended only when the full freighter finally set sail again four days later. This first extended stay heralded the kind of impact my life would have on this continent's soon-to-be independent country of Kenya.

The *Robin Gray*, with my small family aboard, continued

its voyage up the eastern coast of Africa stopping at other ports, each time witnessing the poor treatment of the Africans by their abusive bosses. I vividly recall our stop at the port of Beira, Province of Mozambique, where I witnessed a scene I will never forget. At this time Mozambique was controlled by the Portuguese, and the Portuguese business bosses used the locals to load heavy ore onto the cargo ships. One of the African workers had a piece of ore thrown at him, which hit his back. I was reminded of Peter the Apostle's command not to lord it over those entrusted to your care. I was beginning to see we had a lot of hard work ahead of us. The boundaries among the Cape Coloreds, the Blacks, and the Whites were as hard as ice—Apartheid was in their blood. Not even the warm ocean beaches thawed the separations, as each group could not so much as swim within 300 feet of each other in the spacious Indian Ocean.

The forty-one day voyage across the Atlantic and around the Horn of Africa provided plenty of time for me to reflect on my life up to this point. What had happened in my life that made me fearless to move my young, growing family halfway around the globe for an undetermined length of time at a time when the latest communication device was the tethered Princess phone and my home country had just expanded westward with the addition of Alaska into the union? The one and only answer was faith—faith in Jesus Christ from first to last!

REFLECTION QUESTION:
*What major decision did you make in your life
based on faith alone?*

CHAPTER 2

My Childhood

My life's voyage began twenty-three years earlier on January 4, 1936, when my brother Robert and I were born in New York City to Paul and Catherine Johansson. Apparently, the double blessing of twins was not enough for my petite mother Catherine because at the end of that same calendar year my sister Gladys, later known as Gigi, was born. It was not until five more years passed that my dear mother delivered my second sister Marilyn and another two-and-a-half years before the birth of my youngest sister Carol.

My father, Paul, was a devoted Christian man who faithfully drove our old 1933 Chevy at least 40 miles round trip for the first decade of nearly forty years of work at the *Newsday*. As one of the charter members of the largest newspaper on Long Island, Dad also served as a printer. The type of job my father worked didn't really matter as long as he could provide for his family of seven. This ministry of providing well for his family built a solid foundation for Dad's desire to provide for hungry souls outside our family as well, therefore, he faithfully served as a Sunday school superintendent for some twenty-five or thirty years at Community Gospel Tabernacle (later Evangel Church) in Astoria, Queens.

Mom and Dad didn't make much money, but that did not stop them from giving a large percentage of their income to missions. One lasting financial agreement between my dad and my mom was giving to missions and pledging to missions by faith. This agreement left little money for the finer things in life like brand new furniture, so for their 25th wedding anniversary my siblings and I bought them a brand new living room set. Mom said it was her first *new* thing and, surprisingly, she did not have an attitude about it or quote her oft proclaimed belief: "Son, you know, we believe Jesus Christ is coming soon, and I don't want to leave any furniture for the antichrist." In fact, she was very pleased; I could tell from her delightful smile. She was a giver and not a taker, but she embraced the opportunity to practice receiving in this situation. Both Dad and Mom spoke of their gratefulness for this brand new gift.

My mom Catherine organized her children effectively each and every school morning, while Dad was away at work. Since there were no big, yellow school buses to transport us to and from school, Mom made sure we were prepared for the mile long trek to the highly integrated PS 127 in Queens. I remember one time my mother witnessed Rob and me fighting with a bunch of boys who outnumbered us. She quickly sprang into action, letting those other boys have you know what! My mother was a chip off the old block of her dad. I still think my brother and I could have handled the situation ourselves, but Mom was not going to take any chances. In addition to being very positive, she was very protective.

> *Son, you know we believe Jesus Christ is coming soon, and I don't want to leave any furniture for the antichrist.*

Besides home, another place of safety for me and my siblings was church. In fact, at times my brother Robert and I entered into the peace and rest of Jesus so deeply that we would fall asleep under the pews while the services rolled on to the tunes our mother joyously plucked out on the piano. At other times, Rob and I lost the peace and rest of Jesus to the point we wrestled in the back row of the sanctuary. Once when this happened, Gramps, who was also our pastor, called us up on the platform to sit perfectly still looking out over the audience members as they stared back at us, everyone being fully aware of our misbehavior! This was how we were first exposed to being called up on the platform, but it wasn't to be the speakers, yet. This way Rob and I learned early on to look at people from the point of view of the platform and, as children, we had our own unique point of view concerning Gramps, my brother, and me while up on the platform. Since we each sat in one of three chairs on the platform, we imagined Gramps as the Father seated on his throne, me as the Son seated at his right hand, and my brother as the ever-present Holy Ghost.

While I experienced safety at home and church, my childhood was far from sheltered beyond that, which provided for some great life lessons providentially designed by my heavenly Father. One lesson I learned at an early age was—Don't hold onto cherished possessions tightly because they could disappear in a flash. If Mom didn't want money spent on new furniture, imagine her aversion to the growing national fascination with the television set, so riding my bike in nice weather outdoors filled space in my time that otherwise would have been spent watching *Howdy Doody* or *The Three Stooges*. To Mom then, an expensive lambswool bicycle seat cover seemed more a necessity than a luxury Christmas gift to help keep a thirteen-year-old occupied. One day I rode my luxury cushioned-seat Schwinn down to the nearby bay to dig clams. The best clam digging was across the water on the sandbar. When the tide went out, I would step across the water on big, smooth rocks to get to the clam-diggers' paradise. One particular time, though, I no sooner situated myself on the other shore when, from across the water, I saw someone taking my expensive bicycle seat cover. I knew I didn't have enough time to catch the thief because the expanse of water with the rock steps was between us. This incident reinforced my belief I couldn't assume all people were trustworthy, especially in the city. It also taught me a truth I have embraced my entire life—Cherished possessions cannot be held onto too tightly, prompting me to always keep my hands held wide open, palm sides up. Furthermore, this very incident furthered my belief I would not be defined by possessions. I was still the same young man who was rich in Christ, despite being poor in luxury bicycle seat covers.

Another life lesson I learned in childhood and held onto my entire life was—The world is full of temptations I am able to resist by God's strength. By the time I reached high school age,

I was expected to be responsible enough to decide which high school I wanted to attend. I decided to enroll in an all-boys school for graphic arts—the New York School of Printing. This Manhattan school was located in three places: the main school located on floors 13, 14, and 15 of a building at the corner of Eighth Avenue and 34th Street; an old building (a former Civil War hospital) on 35th Street; and the third location at Ninth and 29th Street. In order to attend the school's mandatory gym classes, we boys had to walk about five city blocks from the school's one location at the corner of Eighth and 34th to the Ninth and 29th Street YMCA through city streets generously infused with gangs, drugs, and other temptations. At that time, the area from 42nd Street to 34th Street had deteriorated into a haunt of hundreds of adult bookstores and palm readers' shops. On my way to gym, I even had to walk by fliers, cards, and advertisements for the local prostitutes. It was like a war zone. Each day

> *The world is full of temptations I am able to resist by God's strength.*

when I returned home from school, I threw my school books on my bed and knelt down to thank God for bringing me through that day victoriously. I never once went into any of the tempting businesses. Over time, the temptations weakened as I gained strength from my daily practice. I am deeply grateful for the strong, foundational Christian principles steeped into me at home, which helped me to survive this kind of battle so early on in my life.

One summer day when I was about fourteen years old, my grandfather Williams (aka Gramps) wisely suggested that my parents loosen up a bit and take a vacation, so my parents surprisingly announced they wanted to take the whole family of seven on a vacation. My parents didn't have a deep bank account to tap into, but Mom's father Gramps led us to tap into our God-given creativity. Gramps had a flatbed trailer and hitch on the back of his Hudson. Surely his 5-foot by 8-foot trailer and matching hitch could be transformed into something useful for an all-out vacation he reasoned. In just two days, Dad, utilizing his own well-developed discipline and Mom's can-do encouragement, transformed that flatbed into a useful camper travel trailer until off we went. Mom had kept declaring to Dad, "Paul, we can do this!" Dad had believed her and had continued to build our one-room box onto Gramps' utility trailer using Masonite boards. This creation didn't have much aesthetic appeal, but it sure did do its job. Inside he installed two bunks—one up high for Rob and me and another split bunk underneath with an aisle in between for Mom and Gigi. On the floor of the aisle laid a full mattress for Dad to sleep flanked by my two youngest sisters, Marilyn and Carol. Our upper bunk had heavy-duty hinges attached for easy fold up. Summers in New York State can be quite warm and that summer was one of them. Since our camper lacked an air conditioner, or even any windows, my brother and I were having trouble breathing inside it. We problem solved by cutting a square hole in the side wall and attaching a couple of hinges for easy opening and closing of the cutout piece. Now we had a window! More proof that Mom's encouraging words to Dad during this whole creation were true. We could do it. This was modus operandi for Rob and me while growing up. Whenever my brother and I noticed we lacked something, we followed Gramps' example and just created it. We were never poor this way because Gramps taught us we could create what was lacking. We even created bicycles just by going to a junkyard, finding parts, and reassembling them. It was just us two boys, made in the image of our Creator, creating like He does.

We pulled out of New York City and drove around our entire home state in Gramps' Hudson pulling our homemade camper. Some of my favorite destinations were Ausable Chasm, Howe Caverns, Niagara Falls, Letchworth State Park, and Watkins Glen State Park. The whole family had a great and memorable time on this two-week long trip. When we returned home, we disassembled the temporary camper, turning it back into a simple flatbed. A third lesson I learned from my childhood was—Don't ever say, "I can't do it." These were words I *never* heard my mom say together—"I" and "can't"—even when it came to living in a Masonite box on wheels for two weeks. It was into this world I was born and raised that destined me to choose to creatively serve the Lord with my whole heart for the rest of my life with a fearless, compassionate heart for the City.

REFLECTION QUESTION:

What key lifelong lessons have you learned from your childhood?

CHAPTER 3

Gramps

My maternal grandfather, Evan Williams, pioneered and pastored the church our family faithfully attended. His wife Anna, affectionately called "Nana," was a caring and loving wife. He was a leader, and she allowed him to lead. They had seven children, all of whom eventually came to know the Lord Jesus personally. Gramps learned the hard way that a pastor's children are sheep who need their father's time as much, if not more, than the sheep at church, so by the time Rob and I came along he had that figured out. That is why he spent extra, intentional time including my brother and me in everything he did to help others.

Besides being a great husband and pastor, Gramps was a great builder—a builder of buildings, a builder of vision, and a builder of men. One of his special building projects was called "the prophet's chamber." Gramps saw the need for a private room for missionaries to stay in until their ships set sail from the nearby port. Putting deeds to his faith, he designed and built a slanted roof efficiency apartment complete with a small bathroom and kitchenette at the church. He completed this hospitable package by directing our family to help any missionaries staying there to pack their belongings into boxes, band the boxes (he even owned a banding machine for this), and place them in storage until their departure. Finally, when the missionaries were ready to leave, a group of people from church would accompany the missionaries to the dock and send them off singing encouraging chorus' lines like "God be with you till we meet again at Jesus' feet." Missionaries from different organizations steadily stopped by our church on their way to remote corners of the earth. Word of mouth advertising kept the prophet's chamber continuously filled. Sometimes displaced people even moved into the prophet's chamber until we helped them find another place to live. This kind of practical involvement in both foreign and local missions permeated our church life at Community Gospel Tabernacle and provided living models of living by faith in the Son of God for me and my siblings during our highly impressionable years.

Gramps may have been called into full-time ministry, but that did not mean he no longer did any manual labor. In fact, the sweat of his brow melded right into his ministry. His hard work modeled a life ever choosing work to serve ministry (not vice versa) and freed me early on from any entitlement mentality in the ministry. It seemed as though Gramps, my father, and the other men of the church were perpetually completing one kind or another of a building project through our home church. I always looked up to Gramps because he was always a positive, God-fearing example of what it means to be a true man of God.

When he was a full-time contractor in his earlier years, Gramps even built our house at 110-10 Ditmars Boulevard, which was just one of the fifteen or so houses he built on our block. My brother Rob and I spent the first seventeen years of our lives in this house that Gramps built. Perhaps the best aspect of the house was its view overlooking Flushing Bay. For me, looking out the framed windows of our home was like watching a big screen movie before the big screen was common. Airplanes took off and landed at LaGuardia Airport daily right in front of my eyes. When the weather was nice I could savor the view overlooking the beautiful bay full of boats as I swung in our yard's oversized swing. A pleasant, beautiful place at that time, now it is not beautiful at all because the bay is filled with LaGuardia's runways.

One pleasant and beautiful day Gramps found me working down in the cellar of our house. When he inquired as to why I was working inside while it was so nice outside, I described to him a conflict I was having with a kid on the block. He empathized with me just a bit and left. Shortly, he returned through the basement door with a peanut butter and jam sandwich in hand and instructed me to go give it to my "enemy" kid on the block. With trepidation, I obeyed. What had been an irritating situation,

Gramps transformed into a teachable moment for me to learn the principle that to be in charge through godly actions works better than to become subordinate through fleshly reactions.

This lesson from Gramps also taught me the power of sharing my food. So, on the very day the world celebrated the end of enemy fighting during World War II, my friends and I decided to share scoopfuls of delicious, vanilla ice cream door-to-door in our neighborhood. Now the 2-gallon tub of vanilla ice cream we decided to share came into our possession just moments after a passing Mayflower ice cream truck lost the tub through its open back door. At first I thought the lost tub was a toy drum with its cylinder body and drumhead-looking top. Upon closer inspection, I learned, as the former owner's truck's musical trail drifted into the distance, this "drum" was completely full of ice cream. In those days no home in our neighborhood owned a freezer, so I figured the godliest action was to just hurry up and share our food.

Our Ditmars Boulevard home was divided up into the main living quarters downstairs, where Gramps and Nana lived out a great example of what it means to be a Christian couple through extended and frequent prayer meetings, and a shared upstairs apartment where my parents, siblings, and I lived. Gramps built our house when he was in his thirties and, by the end of his thirties, he had stepped down from his construction business altogether in order to serve God full time. Reminiscing about this house that Gramps built provides so many bittersweet memories, but one of the saddest memories was the day Gramps moved out to the church apartment 4 miles away and we moved down—downstairs into the more spacious living quarters. I missed having Gramps literally right underneath my feet.

As a child I wondered if there was anything Gramps couldn't do. Believing in the power of a gracious and good God, one time Gramps even prayed and fasted for twenty-one days for a woman whose body was troubled by a huge tumor on her stomach and whose spirit was tormented by evil. She was one of his sheep who always came late to services and put a damper on the meetings through her distractions. After two full weeks of fasting for this one woman, Gramps' pants loosened so much he had to tie them up with a rope. After three weeks of Gramps' fasting, this tormented woman came in late to service, made a scene, and sat down in the second row. Gramps reached out his hand and said, "In the name of Jesus, be healed." She was completely healed in less than a minute. She spent the rest of her life calling people listed in the New York City telephone book to explain how much God loves them (she never got out of the last names beginning with the letter A). I have witnessed the reality of God's life-changing, miracle power working through my own grandfather.

I never got to know my paternal grandpa Axel Johansson because he died a few years after I was born. What I did learn about him was that he first came to the United States as a seaman on a boat from Sweden. The conditions of the trip were so difficult, he arrived with frostbitten hands. Despite the difficulty, he was able to use those hands in his new country to become foreman of a Bell Telephone Company crew that dug holes for and set telephone poles. From what I understand, my dad seemed to take after his dad in many ways like holding the line on his beliefs, remaining very faithful to job and family, and appearing alarmingly strong.

REFLECTION QUESTION:

Who influenced your life the way Gramps influenced my life?

CHAPTER 4

Camp Bethel

After Gramps moved onto the church property, he had a big idea to bring people together for community outside the City, so he led Community Gospel Church to obtain a 13-acre piece of property for building a Christian camp some 50 miles south of New York City at Old Bridge, New Jersey. At that time property in this undeveloped part of New Jersey could be obtained by a sort of homesteading. All we had to do was rope off the land we wanted for a year, clear it, and start building. We used long elevator cables from New York City to rope off our desired land for the one year. After one full year no one else claimed our roped-off land, so it became ours. My dad was one of the original homesteaders of a small piece of property from the perimeter of this site where we built a little summer home for our family to enjoy the true outdoors without the concrete and congestion that came with the density of population in the Big Apple. After all of Gramps' Christian friends who wanted a place at Old Bridge settled in, Camp Bethel (as Gramps named it) spread out over 21 acres with a small creek running along one edge.

Well, our Old Bridge summer home started out more like a bunkhouse than an estate house. It had absolutely no insulation, which made any summer breeze like a welcome breath of fresh air sent straight through from heaven. Each family who settled a small plot of property around the edges of the camp built similar bunk homes. During all the summers our family spent at Old Bridge, Dad still worked on Long Island for the five weekdays, while Mom, with limited help, oversaw my brother and sister and me at camp until Dad returned for the weekends.

Even though Dad was away at work on Long Island during the weekdays, his force was still felt at camp. When I think of our summer home in New Jersey I think of chicken farming—not because we raised chickens at camp, but because of something quite different. Between the ages of two and five, in order to keep my brother and me from wandering into the nearby creek, Mom needed Dad's help, so he built a 3-foot high (quickly extended to a 6-foot high) chicken fence pen around the perimeter of our little yard. Although we never did raise any chickens, my brother and I knew why country folk built chicken yards for safety purposes!

This was enough to keep us in the safety zone of our property by day, but earlier on Mom needed something more to keep us children safe inside our camp house at night. That is why Dad built the crow's nest-like structure in our bedroom where my brother and I could safely sleep or imagine ourselves inside the lookout of a ship. Our unique twin bed jutted out from our bedroom wall approximately 3 feet down from the ceiling. I think of it as a twin bed not because there was just enough room for one person, but because my dad designed the 2-foot wide by 7-foot long bed to fit both my twin brother and me inside on top of perfectly fitting little mattresses. A single chicken wire door was padlocked on the front side to keep us from falling the 5 feet to the floor and doubly to ensure we kept away from the added danger of the nearby creek. The only sailing we could do with this set-up was in our dreams. Gigi's crib was efficiently tucked right in underneath our crow's nest. Mom slept peacefully while Dad was away, knowing her rambunctious boys were kept safe inside the efficiently handmade bunk bed for twins.

> *"Camp Bethel made men for ministry!"*

Once our bunkhouse was completed, my brother and I were expected to help build the main camp building at Camp Bethel, Old Bridge. This experience was like enrolling in a Christian vocational school where we honed our construction skills, while serving the Lord's purposes 24/7. The camp played a big role in forming my brother's and my building skills and gave us opportunities to grow up with a love of the outdoors. Years later

Gramps told us, "Camp Bethel made men for ministry!" Those words could not be truer.

It was a one hour drive one way from Community Gospel Church to Camp Bethel. Dad organized teams of men from church who traveled down on weekends with him to the Old Bridge property to help make Gramps' big idea a reality. As usual, a lot of strong men rallied around Gramps to help create this Christian camp. Each summer day my brother Robert, Gramps, and I prepared everything ahead of time for Dad's weekend teams, and Gramps told us what to do. Ahead of time, Gramps organized everything from scythes, sickles, and hedge trimmers to buckets, poles, and whitewash. Full preparation was a necessity. Everything had to be ready so no one from Dad's teams was standing around wasting time.

The first big assignment at Old Bridge for Rob and me was to put all the tools together in preparation for the men who would come to cut down the useless trees to clear the land. Next, we used a long pole with a brush on the end to whitewash a mark on the best trees Gramps chose to remain on the property for both beauty and shade. Every remaining tree was trimmed up to eye level to provide a clear view around the entire camp acreage. We all worked like crazy all day. Every man even had his own file to sharpen his sickle so he could keep on working efficiently even after his blade had been dulled by its constant use. To keep these hearty volunteers' energy levels high, a cook was found to feed these hungry lumbermen and cold water was at their constant disposal.

One morning Gramps switched Rob's and my morning work assignment from voluntary manual laborer to voluntary cook after we asked him what we were going to eat for breakfast that day. Without giving any specific instructions, Gramps left us alone in his cabin to create breakfast. Soon Gramps returned and asked us where breakfast was. We told him there was nothing there from which to make breakfast, so we had done nothing. Knowing God's ability to call things that are not as though they were, Gramps taught us an invaluable lesson that day. He opened up the kitchen cupboard to reveal a single can of clams and a lonely jar of wheat germ. "We have so much food in here!" Gramps proclaimed prior to helping us fry up some delicious "clam fritters" for our breakfast. I realized I had missed seeing the plenty right under my nose until Gramps pointed it out.

Once the land was cleared, our next assignment at Old Bridge was to build a big tabernacle out of wood from Jeep shipping crates salvaged from a nearby dump in New Jersey. First, we boys had to remove all of the nails in the salvaged boards Gramps wanted to use for the building and as high-altitude planks. Before the long planks went up, Gramps instructed Rob and me to place each salvaged board across two cement blocks to be tested for soundness near the ground where no one could get hurt. We then stood in the middle of each and every plank and jumped as hard as we could to try and break them. When we found a board that did not break, Gramps shouted, "Yes!" and instructed us, "Put it on the rope and send it up." In order for Gramps to get from one truss to another, he consecutively placed one of his tested planks between the bottom chords of two standing trusses in order to make a walkway across. Gramps confidently walked across the trustworthy planks from one truss to another because, while a plank may have had a sag in it, it had been proven safe 9 inches from the ground. That is how he confidently walked like a trapeze artist from one truss to another about 20 feet above the ground on salvaged planks my brother and I had tested. It was during this project I noticed another life lesson—If you don't break 9 inches from the ground, you won't break 20 feet in the air. Not only did Gramps model how to lead men in unity, but he also inspired me with a bucketful of analogies, including this one, that I was able to use in training other men and women for the ministry over the years. I have only good memories of the good meetings that took place in that tested tabernacle during the Latter Rain Movement.

Eventually Dad upgraded our bunkhouse, transforming it into a much nicer getaway for Mom and the rest of us. He also eventually freed us from the confines of our room, yard, and property when he bought us a 7-foot long row boat to paddle up and down the nearby creek.

When my brother and I were fourteen years old, our grandfather had the wisdom to receive a gift of an old '29 Model A Ford convertible. We named the old Ford "Henry." Rob and I voluntarily worked on old Henry during work breaks at camp until we got him running. With no license plate and no fenders but plenty of fuel, we raced that salvaged Ford all around the New Jersey campground. We also drove Gramps' old Ford dump truck full of loads of sand all around the property until we found the perfect spots to dump the sand to create our very own sand dunes. We did not modify the suspension or build a roll-over cage in the Model A; nevertheless, we ran it like a dune buggy over our homemade sand dunes. Certainly we had our guardian angels watching over us. I realized as an adult our driving style at that time could have killed us and others as we took people for fast rides in the back of the Ford over the sand dunes and through the surrounding woods.

> *If you don't break 9 inches from the ground, you won't break 20 feet in the air.*

Our Model A Ford adventures happened during our rest time between 1:00 p.m. and 4:00 p.m. each day. Gramps knew that everyone needed a daily Sabbath to balance the rigorous schedule on which he kept all volunteers. Because of the sweltering Jersey heat, our daily summer schedule began at about 5:30 a.m. with hard work until 11:00 a.m. We had a nice, long lunch break from 11:00 a.m. to 1:00 p.m. followed by our "rest" time. We finished off each day back at heavy manual labor from 4:00 p.m. until dark when it was cooler.

I did not realize it at the time, but I was beginning to experience the heavy weight of responsibility and the bird's-eye view of circumstances that grow as you rise in leadership. After we had worked hard for just one whole week at this camp practically killing ourselves, disgruntled guests began to complain about the camp. Here we were just trying to make a go of it, and people who considered themselves "spiritual" because of their "gift of criticism" added a layer of heaviness to our work. I later realized these people were really immature and not spiritually gifted at all. These people ended up doing me a special, unexpected favor because through them I learned early on how to handle the murmuring crowd the way Moses did. At the time I did not see these experiences as leadership development lessons, but I see now that is what they really were.

After my 101 summer leadership development at Camp Bethel, I left with a better understanding of what may be accomplished with hard work, knowing there will always be grumblers whose voices I need not give a lot of weight to, remembering all I need to do is focus on the end result, press on, and do what God wants *me* to do. None of my experiences were a waste of time because God always improved my leadership skills through all of them so I could pass on what I learned to others. I fondly recall those long summer days building at Old Bridge as especially creative and fun for my brother and me. I am convinced more than ever that whatever God calls a person to do can be made creative, interesting, and fun.

REFLECTION QUESTION:

How have you been tested "9 inches from the ground"
to prepare you for "20 feet in the air"?

CHAPTER 5
Elim

No, my first faith assignment outside my hometown of New York City was not to a sunny oasis of twelve springs and seventy palm trees, but the place was named after the biblical oasis recorded in Exodus 15:27 and provided for me an immersion into deep living water and spiritual refreshment. Instead of palm trees, there were oak and maple trees on the Lima, New York, property Elim Bible Institute purchased from the Wesleyan Methodists in 1951. Elim Bible Institute was founded in 1924 by Reverend Ivan Q. Spencer, who led the school into the blessings of the Holy Spirit and participation in the cross of Jesus Christ. Elim's revival roots grafted right into this Lima location on a hill originally built by faith in 1832 by followers of Charles Finney and the 1830 to 1831 revival he led not far away in Rochester, New York.

In 1953 I graduated from the New York School of Printing with highest honors in the vocational tract. It was now time for me to make another important life decision. Should I accept the major scholarship I was offered for training at the Mergenthaler School of Linotype, which would enable me to follow in the footsteps of my dad in the printing trade? Or, should I go into training for full-time ministry like Gramps? I was at a crossroads. By example, my father had given my brother and me faithfulness, but my grand-father had given us faith in action. Neither road toward training looked bad or wrong for me. By the grace of God, I chose to train full-time for Christian ministry. I have no regrets about this decision even after the passage of over six decades. I had no idea at the time I made this Spirit-led decision that just three decades later the Mergenthaler Linotype machines would be retired into museums! Certainly, I believe ministry may be fulfilled in the marketplace, but I knew in my heart right then *my* fulfillment was full-time ministry in the USA or full-time on the foreign mission field.

Once again, Gramps played a role in my faith development. It was through my home church I heard about Elim and launched out into my first big faith assignment. In the early 1950s, Gramps led our congregation toward both foreign missions and a new move of God. This new move brought liberty from bondage as well as spiritual renewal for members of our church, especially my parents. During this divine move of God, all of the college-aged youth at church, including my brother, sister, two of my aunts, and me, chose to attend Elim Bible Institute because the school wholeheartedly embraced this fresh move of God. Since my brother, my Aunt Jenette Williams, and I were not yet eighteen years old in 1953, Gramps had to drive our 1941 Chevy through the Holland Tunnel into New Jersey before returning home and sending the three of us, more than old enough to drive outside New York City, forward into the remainder of the 300 mile journey to our oasis.

My brother Rob and I got off to a good start with the new Dean of Men Elmer Frink when we first arrived at Elim. Rob and I decided we had waited long enough in the lounge for the new Dean of Men Frink to arrive and assign us our room, so we decided to go ahead and find the best room in this main building for ourselves. We found a spacious room on the fourth floor and moved right in similar to the way Gramps had taught us to rope off the land we wanted in Old Bridge. Instead of using elevator cables to draw our boundary lines, we just moved all of our personal belongings right into the room we had chosen. Dean Frink eventually came by and asked us what we were doing. We told him possession was ninety percent of the law so we had possessed our room. We had learned well from Gramps! Well, Dean Frink laughed a good belly laugh with us and placed his stamp of approval on our claim.

The school had just moved onto its Lima property, which provided for a plethora of possibilities to help offset the cost of my brother's and my Elim tuition. My work assignment was as the school's official printer. Paying attention to my father's printing trade and the Holy Spirit's leading made the way for me to land and develop at this post for my full three-year stay. Using the latest in printing technology, the offset printer, I printed a small monthly magazine and all of the school forms. I even built a dark room that functioned like a giant camera body. When I walked into this camera body room, I could photograph outside the room using a 2-inch diameter camera lens installed into the wall. All I had to do to enlarge or reduce the print was to move the copy on the glass forward or backward and then develop the negative to make an offset plate for printing.

Elim proved a safe place where I could spread my wings. One day Rob and I were invited to round up heifers at an off-campus farm. I did not know one thing about dairy farming, but I did know something about "chicken farming," so we unreservedly jumped into the large farm truck and rode off campus to the side of a big pasture. Dave Larkin, the man in charge of the farm, instructed us to round up the herd of heifers one by one by placing our fingers up their noses, squeezing, and pulling the beasts up into the truck bed until all ten were aboard. Blood ran down my hands and under my fingernails as I cowed all ten disgruntled bovine onto the truck. Somehow we all made it back to campus where we went through a similar process to unload the cows into the barn at the farm the school maintained. I had read nothing in any Elim handbook about becoming a real urban cowboy as part of Elim training, but apparently my heavenly Father thought it was another perfect assignment. A real farm, complete with barn and silo, had come with the original Elim property. Since Elim's founder Ivan Q. Spencer grew up a farmer, he was experienced enough to continue to maintain the farm. Ivan was really happy with Elim's farm because he could care for cows at the same time he cared for God's people. He even asked me to build a roof and a loading door on the new brick silo to keep the grain for the cows dry.

Another time I was sent to the school's barn to help Dave Larkin deliver a calf by breech birth. Dave had his arm all the way inside the cow when he turned the breech calf inside right-side up. Together we pulled the calf out along with gushing blood and guts! Both calf and mother cow lived. Imagine coming out of New York City and taking this as a job!

Without a doubt, the most important circumstance at Elim was meeting a young lady who came to the school at the same time I did. One day early on in my time at Elim, I looked into the dining room and spotted the most beautiful young lady I had ever seen cleaning tabletops for her practical duty assignment. Her beauty and spunk were intriguing, her commitment to Christ inspiring. I wanted to get to know her better and, lo and behold, we providentially ended up that semester at the same Monroe County nursing home outstation ministry. I was beginning to see our united potential was from God. Our relationship developed slowly over the next few years. There it was at Elim that an outgoing New York boy met, and eventually married, a somewhat reserved Michigan girl. From the start we provided a balance for each other. We shared the added blessing of the freedom to be ourselves without any worry of rejection; therefore, our lives grew and matured both emotionally and spiritually together into a lifetime of full-time service to our God.

While at Elim, before we married, Gloria and I witnessed loving older couples modeling their sacred matrimonial trusts as they served God. For example, Carlton Spencer, the president of the school, with his wife Elizabeth, served God while they raised their family right on campus for all to watch. There was also Reverend Elmer Frink, dean of men and missions teacher, whose godly example deeply impacted my brother and me. Reverend Frink came to Elim as a former widower, since his first wife succumbed to blackwater fever during their service in Nigeria. Upon returning to the United States, he married the beautiful June, who remained his constant companion until his passing parted them. My brother and I knew that this man of God had been tested 9 inches from the ground; therefore, we stood high on his shoulders when we gave him the privilege to speak life into our lives. Elim stamped a lifelong impression into our lives that went way deeper than the buildings and beautiful Upstate New York setting; Elim's impact was eternal.

In November of 1953 I began to earnestly seek the Lord in my heart to give me direction for my future. Soon George Lindsay, a missionary friend, asked me to drive him in my 1941 Chevy some 50 miles away to a missionary meeting where he was speaking. George had just returned from Cuba and was on his way to Kenya. A small group of people gathered at the small church where George spoke and showed a short presentation of slides from Kenya belonging to Brother Carlton Spencer, Elim's founder's son. It was during this slide show I became aware of my personal call to the African field. I had been exposed to foreign missions from the earliest days of my life, but I did not know it was my personal call until this day. I now thought I was personally called to Africa. God was beginning to answer my prayers for direction. Soon, during Elim's annual January week of prayer, I spent all seven days in prayer and fasting for confirmation that this was indeed God's direction for my future. The Holy Spirit assured me that this would be my life's direction, and that week I committed myself to do whatever it would take to fulfill a call to Africa. At that time I thought I would be ministering in the Congo; however, as I allowed God to be God and fill in the details of my call, it became clear that my first step would be to Kenya.

Our '41 Chevy proved useful beyond relocating my aunt, brother, and me to our rural oasis and transporting us around the country for evangelistic meetings; that old car also carried several Elim students to what were called "outstations." Outstations were various ministry locations where Elim students practically applied their abstract classroom learning to real life situations. I distinctly remember my 1953 fall outstation when I drove a team of students south about 100 miles from the school to a church in Elkland, Pennsylvania. The return trip to Elim was what was most memorable and provided the perfect training ground for further development of the deep work of the Holy Spirit's fruit in my life. As I started driving that cold, rainy night, the car threw a rod out the bottom of the engine's oil pan. I was able to roll the car to a nearby garage with a phone and call the pastor from the church we had just visited for help. He and his wife came to our rescue, taking all of us back to his home for the now snowy night. The next morning Burt Roberts, an Elim student from Idaho, brought my brother and picked up all of the stranded students. Rob and I stayed behind to start taking the car apart.

For the next three days Rob and I worked in the snow to remove the head and oil pan off the engine so we could install the used piston my brother had brought. (Did I mention the rain had turned to snow the night our car broke down?) It was a miracle that the used piston was a perfect fit. As I returned to Elim, I realized I had learned another important life lesson—Never fix a car motor outside in the snow! In that same calendar year while I was home for Thanksgiving break, my father bought us a rebuilt six-cylinder block for the Chevy and helped us to change its engine. The three of us—Rob, Jenette, and I—drove back to Elim with a "new" motor. That '41 Chevy transported us back and forth from Lima to NYC without incident for all holidays for two more years until we replaced it in 1955.

The following summer of 1954 my brother and I drove our old '41 Chevy thousands of miles around the eastern United States preaching, showing the film *Venture into Faith* by Oral Roberts, leading altar calls, and praying for the sick. Because we looked younger than our years, many pastors asked us, "Where is the evangelist who is going to speak tonight?" We were more than happy to inform the questioners we were the evangelists before we went right to work setting up the movie projector and preparing for the meetings. We were obeying each and every believer's call to represent Jesus and present His salvation message, and we started right in our home country. By the end of our own venture of faith driving that worn-out Chevy, the car was ready for retirement.

Our replacement car was a 1951 Nash Ambassador. Over the summer of 1955, Rob and I saved enough money not only to pay our school bills, but also to purchase a two-tone, gray six cylinder Nash sedan with overdrive. We worked various jobs that summer in order to save up, but the most challenging job was the one we accepted putting a new roof on a Buffalo, New York, church pastored by Reverend Chester Gretz. Not only did we put new shingles on that church's roof, but we first redesigned the roof and finally replaced the steeple! Soon after our debt-free purchase of the Nash, we discovered on a trip from Buffalo, New York, to Elim that the car needed new pistons since it was burning oil. Now Rob and I had developed some background knowledge about changing pistons from our '41 Chevy experience in the snow. This time, however, we asked permission to work on the engine inside a local gas station during a warm, summer month. We easily tore that engine apart and rebuilt it with new pistons, rings, and inserts. We gave the car a little push, and the engine started right up. We decided then and there we needed to break that engine in, so we proceeded to test drive it by driving to Mexico and back for a total of 6000 miles in three weeks. Wes Moore (aka Tex), my future brother-in-law, rode along with us on our test drive so each one could rotate taking turns driving while the other two passengers slept until we reached El Paso, Texas. We chose El Paso because Tex's parents pastored a church there. For safety purposes, we drove his father's car with a Texas license plate over the border to Juarez, Mexico, and back to El Paso before completing the Nash's engine break-in from El Paso to Lima.

On our return drive home we decided, since we were so close, Tex would drive us over to Carlsbad, New Mexico, to see the caverns. On our way there, suddenly, Tex jammed the brakes right in the middle of a New Mexico highway and pulled over. All three of us jumped out to witness the critter Tex decided to avoid making into road kill. It was a tarantula, which showed up a perfect specimen against the white concrete road. We carefully placed our captured spider into an emptied out paper lunch bag along with a small piece of leftover lettuce and set him inside the bumper end of our car's trunk. Before closing the trunk lid, we made a tiny air hole in the brown bag to provide oxygen for our new travel partner and continued on our way. Before we left on this non-stop driving adventure, we had agreed to quickly stop by Gloria's parents' home in Michigan on our way back to New York to pick up the stuff Gloria would need for her last year at Elim and transport it there. By the time we reached the Michigan border, it was my brother Rob's turn to drive. This time it was Rob who jammed the brakes and rammed the gear shift into neutral right in the middle of the highway. Instantly, we all saw the problem as Rob pointed. There, swinging from the lowest point of the car's key chain located in the ignition, was our fourth hairy passenger. Our tarantula proved a miraculous escape artist who escaped out of the paper bag, squeezed through an unseen hole between the trunk and the back seat, traveled across the prostrate sleeping passenger in the back seat, and scaled the leg of the driver to perform his final entertainment swinging from our car's key chain. We decided to put an end to his escapades inside our car. We recaptured him in the same bag he had escaped from after we taped the small air hole shut.

> *I became enveloped in a light of liquid love.*

Since we learned our tarantula was a real entertainer, we decided to use him for further entertainment value once we arrived in Gloria's neighborhood. There we tied a string around two of the arachnids' legs leaving long strings at both ends to work as reigns. This way our spider could run and play in front of the neighborhood children who had never before seen a tarantula, let alone a "circus" tarantula. The children absolutely loved our little entertainer. We decided the neighborhood children back home in New York City would be just as delighted, so after we dropped Gloria's stuff off in Lima, New York, we traveled home to New York City in hopes of delighting the hearts of more children. We were very disappointed to find the brown bag had become a coffin for our new friend. Wanting to squeeze even more value out of God's creature, we donated his 9-inch leg span remains to a local New York City high school's science laboratory. Life never needs to be dull.

While at Elim in early 1956, I spent some time reading *Hosea: The Heart and Holiness of God* by G. Campbell Morgan. Not long thereafter, I became aware of a light in my dorm room around the midnight hour. The best way I can explain what happened to me was I became enveloped in a light of liquid love. I had a divine encounter. Before this event, I had served God because it was the right thing to do. I had loved God, but now I knew He loved me more no matter what happened to me. Until this time I felt somewhat deserving of His love because of my sacrificial service to Him. But that night changed everything. I now knew if I spit in His face, it would not change His love for me. From that night forward, my service to Him rested solely on His surpassing, irrevocable love for me. Songwriter George Matheson penned my experience well:

> Oh, love that wilt not let me go,
> I rest my weary soul in Thee;
> I give Thee back the life I owe,
> That in Thine ocean depths its flow
> May richer, fuller be.
> That truly is my testimony.

Upon graduation from Elim in early May 1956 until late July of that same year, I traveled in the Elim quartet. The quartet members were Ron Owens, whose father was a missionary in Switzerland; Anthony Petrone, a friend whose father pastored an Italian church in Rochester, New York; my brother Robert; and I. If our '51 Nash Ambassador didn't break down on its test drive to Mexico, I was confident it would prove sound driving our quartet thousands of miles around the country from New York to the top of Maine, from Maine into Canada, from Canada around to the bottom of Virginia, from Virginia to central Indiana, and finally back to New York. So off we traveled to preach the Good News in word and song, to honor our Lord Jesus Christ and to represent Elim Bible Institute. This was no money making venture; we volunteered and took just enough reimbursement to cover our travel expenses during our three-month-long journey. What we didn't receive in money, though, we made up for in the joy of witnessing many young people turn to Christ. We were reaping an eternal reward that no money could buy! The only problem was I did need some money for my upcoming marriage to Gloria. I knew from watching my dad and Gramps that a man provided for his own family, despite his calling; otherwise, he denied the faith.

Once again, Gramps proved faithful. In late summer (the quartet had disbanded toward the end of July 1956) I returned to the City and asked Gramps if he knew of anyone who had a job I could do for just eight weeks. By "chance" at that exact time, he knew a woman who needed the windows serviced on an apartment building she owned on Broadway. He described the job as one where I would clean windows, repaint any chipping areas, and putty in the cracks of the window frames where the glass was about to fall out onto Broadway. Beginning on the top 13th floor, I worked my way down one or two floors in eight weeks. Since the woman had no external scaffolding, I jury-rigged an inch-and-a-quarter rope around the inside radiator of each room and back through a big, heavy belt tied around my waist. Using this apparatus I was easily able to lean out of the many windows to do my job. I imagine I looked like a small upper sail on a frigate. I was paid $100 per week for eight weeks for a whopping total of $800. By the time my wedding day arrived in November, I had the whole cash sum stuffed in my pocket. My net worth may have been just $800, but my heavenly worth was about to increase exponentially when I added my beautiful bride to my side.

It was November 10, 1956, in Jackson, Michigan. The outdoor temperature hovered in a range just above 40 degrees. Inside the Calvary Methodist Church the warm fellowship of the three pastors—Gloria's pastor Brother Taylor, my grandfather Pastor Evan Williams, and Reverend Elmer Frink—tied the knot of eternal love around us. Both Gloria's family and my family joined us to serve as witnesses along with the third person of the triune God. If a threefold cord could not easily be broken, then surely three three-fold cords—one of three holy pastors, another of several family witnesses, and the third of the Holy Trinity—absolutely would never be broken!

Immediately, we set out in our Nash for our tri-state honeymoon trip around Lake Michigan. We started and finished in Jackson, Michigan, located in the south-central part of the state. During our weeklong journey that peaked at the upper peninsula, we also stopped in Chicago, Illinois; Milwaukee, Wisconsin; and even crossed the newly opened suspension bridge at St. Ignace, Michigan.

Upon returning from our honeymoon, we stopped by Gloria's parents' home where we loaded up the Nash with our wedding gifts and proceeded to drive straight through on Route 6 from Jackson, Michigan, to Meshoppen, Pennsylvania. This little borough near Scranton in eastern Pennsylvania was the location of our first ministry assignment as the newlywed Johanssons at a small pioneer church founded just one year earlier by a female evangelist. At first we rented a house in which to live from this founding evangelist some nine-and-a-half miles away in Mahoopany; however, we soon moved right into "downtown" Meshoppen and closer to the church in order for the people to get to know us. How could we authentically reach the town unless the townspeople witnessed our lives and we built close relationships?

When we first arrived in town I took a job with the Whipple Lumber Company in Lacey's Hill, Pennsylvania. I enjoyed the job because it was an honorable way to provide for my wife and me, and I could practice the building trade Gramps had so carefully taught me. This time I was not helping Gramps to build a Christian camp; I was now building large picture windows for homes. Although building again appealed to me, I quit after only two weeks. I thought: If I am serving God full-time seventy to eighty hours per week, will He not supply adequate finances for certainly "the worker deserves his wages" (I Tim. 5:18b)?

God did, indeed, supply adequate finances for us at this time through mysterious means and unexpected methods. Our adequate unexpected methods began when we planted a garden for food and chopped wood for heat, finishing up through the very right hand and holy arm of God who gave us the strength to persevere. In addition, many times we opened our back door mysteriously finding a bagful of food for the day. Sometimes bananas and a roast were provided. Both Gloria and I grew in our understanding of hard work and trusting God simultaneously when our hard work appeared not to be adequate. For instance, one day Gloria informed me we had no food in the house. I asked her if we had at least any potatoes, to which she replied in the affirmative. I responded, "This is good! We will make potato soup." We never, ever went without food; it seemed we had tapped into an endless supply. It just didn't always come in the expected way. The question became for us—"Can we serve the Lord joyfully even if we have very limited finances and cannot yet see the supply?" I now know for sure the answer was a resounding—"Yes!" Faith became more than an abstract concept; it became our lifeline. This was perfect training for the lifestyle and challenges God would call us to in the next season of our life together.

Another unexpected way God subsidized our expenses was through a flexible job at the local Chrysler dealership. We took absolutely no finances from the church where we were serving, so I had to do something. My earlier experiences working long hours under the hood of our '51 Nash just to keep it running supplied me with the exact skills needed at the dealership. They hired me whenever they needed brakes redone, transmissions rebuilt, and general tuneups performed.

One day at the dealership, I was standing donned in grease-laden old jeans and a junky shirt underneath the lift greasing a car when the local, well-dressed Free Methodist pastor walked up to me. He informed me a local woman had recently passed away and he wanted me to help him with her funeral. My mind immediately wandered back to my recent visit with this elderly woman. I recalled going into her house where I learned she had been bedridden for fourteen long years. Upon seeing my youthful appearance, the woman had greeted me with these words:

"Sonny, what does a young man like you know about suffering?" I felt immediate compassion for her and the Holy Spirit impressed upon me to respond: "I know nothing about suffering, but I bring to you One who knows everything about suffering for He died on a cruel cross." She was so deeply moved at these life-giving words and subsequent prayer for her, she handed me two dollars when I went to leave. This was Gloria's grocery money for the week! My wife was so excited we would now be able to eat, she went right out and spent the entire two dollars on groceries. After this pleasant remembrance, the smell of lithium grease awakened my senses and my mind returned to the Free Methodist pastor's request. I joyfully accepted the pastor's invitation to share at this charitable woman's funeral service.

Now that woman's two dollar gift may not sound like much money even for that time, but it was all of the unseen provision attached to those two little dollar bills that was so rich. I was paid $20 for speaking at that generous woman's funeral—ten times the amount she had handed me in life. That was not the end of the story, though. This recently deceased woman even left a $200 gift for the church in her will. That money was used to buy property for the church. This was just one of the many memorable funeral services that provided me opportunities to invest eternal benefits into the souls of almost every person in and around town, while I reaped some much needed benefits back. Simple experiences like this grew Gloria's and my faith in God from glory to glory believing for the impossible.

Another funeral where I had the privilege of sharing a simple message of comfort and salvation came as an unpleasant surprise. An eight-year-old, redheaded boy from a very dysfunctional family lived on a mountain at the edge of town. Gloria and I had led this youngster to accept Jesus Christ as his Savior during one of our Vacation Bible Schools. Thereafter, every time we saw this boy, he would ask, "Is the 'tooch' going to be open today?", which further endeared him to our hearts. One day I was away from home serving at a youth camp when word came to me that this little boy had set a match to a 50-gallon gasoline drum while playing at the local fireman's carnival. The drum exploded and the boy caught fire. On his deathbed, that young boy asked for me. It didn't take me long to drive the 170 miles from the camp to the hospital. The staff stood aside while I spent time at the bedside of this boy who had been burned beyond recognition. Up to this point the town hadn't considered Gloria and me too important, but after this boy's funeral many town's people asked me to speak at their funerals. I now understood how important funerals were to spreading the message of the Gospel to the living. I spoke at five funerals in the two years I lived there.

During our season at Meshoppen, Gloria and I visited Elim for various conferences and camp meetings. It was during one of those visits that Elim founder Ivan Q. Spencer met me on a sidewalk and mentioned the need for a missionary to oversee a mission station some 600 miles inland from the coast of Kenya. I learned the station was located in Bukuria, the center of the Wakuria tribe. At this time, the women of the tribe, for the most part, wore nothing on top. This would be a great departure from any of my cultural experiences thus far I thought. Elim missionaries Roy and Teresa Hill had begun this full-gospel work amongst the Wakuria back in the 1940s. Gloria and I soon accepted the invitation with the understanding we would ultimately go to Nairobi, the urban capital of Kenya. In order for us to follow through on our commitment, we needed to raise a lot of support.

Gloria and I began backtracking among some of the many churches I had made connections with during my time in the quartet two years earlier. We knew it was time to hand the little church at Meshoppen over to someone new since we had not enough time to both travel around the northeastern United States and shepherd God's people. In August 1958 Pastor Saied Adour was installed into the pastorate at Meshoppen.

REFLECTION QUESTION:

Have you experienced a refreshing oasis like Elim?

Axel & Mini Johansson

Evan & Anna Williams

Rob and Paul at the pump

The family with the home-made camper

*Camp Bethel
'29 Model A Ford*

First car: '41 Chevy

*Paul and Rob
with sister, Gigi*

*Paul at Elim
printing press*

Elim College Hall

Paul & Gloria at EBI

Elim Quartet

Mom & Dad Johansson

Graduation 1956 with Grandpa & Nana

Graduation 1956 with Mom & Dad

Johansson Family: Robert, Marilyn, Carol, Gigi, Paul, Mom & Dad

SECTION II
GLORIA

CHAPTER 6
My Early Years

I was born on March 28, 1935, into a Christian family. Well, my parents Llewellyn and Virginia Smith had not been Christians for long at the time of my birth, but it was long enough to impact my entire life, especially since I decided also to accept Jesus Christ as my Lord and Savior. I never did have an exact date marking when I was "born again" into God's forever family; I just know it happened around the age of five or six. There are plenty of people around the world who have no exact marked days of physical birth, yet they know for sure they were born at some point in time. It is the same way with my spiritual birth; I am not quite sure when and where it all started, but it did. Even though I do not remember the exact time or exact age I accepted Jesus as my personal Savior, I do possess an official document marking when I was baptized in water at Loomis Park Baptist Church in 1942 at seven years of age.

My natural family consisted of ten people total—Dad and Mom; Ronnie, Jerry, and me; and then my five younger sisters. In order of birth, my junior sisters are Darlene born in 1938, Margaret Ann born in 1941 and passed away of leukemia in 1942, Carolyn born in 1942, Sandra born in 1944, and Dianne born in 1946. While the Second World War geared up and wound down around the globe, my mother did her own gearing up and winding down in the local hospital's delivery room.

We lived in Jackson, Michigan, in a two-story, single-family house owned by my maternal grandmother. After Margaret Ann's short life of just thirteen months, there were only nine of us to share our home's three bedrooms and one bath. My sister Darlene and I slept in one double bed in the girls' bedroom, while Carolyn slept alone for about two years in a small, single bed next to ours until Sandy was old enough to move out of the crib in Mom and Dad's bedroom and into the opposite end of Carolyn's bed. There they peacefully slept toes to nose and nose to toes. Sandy lost the crib in Mom and Dad's room after the birth of my youngest sister Dianne. Ronnie and Jerry, my two older brothers, had the third bedroom to themselves. The single bathroom had no shower; instead, it had a spacious porcelain clawfoot tub. Because there were so many of us girls, we did not have the luxury of unshared bath time either, so every Saturday night Darlene and I shared a bath besides a bed. Then, as part of my volunteer work as Mom's right hand helper, I would head up bathing my three youngest sisters all at once! Afterward, I even styled their hair in pin curls to ready them for church the next morning. I really enjoyed wrapping each bunch of hair around my finger and driving a bobbie pin across every flat curl to hold it over night. This method of pin curling created beautiful, bouncy tubes of hair for church and provided a way for me to practice heading up my very own "hair salon." Crowded bedrooms and a busy bathroom were all we knew, so it was no problem; it was home.

I attended grades kindergarten through 6 at Trumbull Elementary School. Since we did not have to be at this school until 9:00 a.m., I was able to sleep in until 7:00 a.m. before I needed to get up and get ready for school. I also needed time to plan how to bundle up when the weather was bad because we walked to and from school in all kinds of inclement weather. All during my public school years the girls were required to wear dresses to school. There were times during the winter when the temperature fell so low and the wind blew so strong, the backs of my and my sisters' exposed legs between the bottom of our skirts and the tops of our bobby socks would crack and bleed from the battering. We really didn't mind, though, because we children enjoyed the winter by going sledding, skiing, and ice skating at the Loomis Park rink.

Dad had apprenticed as a tool and die maker and was able to work his trade at the same automobile manufacturing job right up until his retirement. Dad always left for work at 5:45 a.m.

sharp to work at Sparks-Withington Co. right in Jackson. This marked the beginning of Mom's prayer time until we children got up and got ready for school. I remember hearing Mom pray to the point of tears for each of us individually. Although Mom had witnessed all of us children getting "saved" over and over again by going forward at the many altar calls in our Baptist church, Mom could see the very real everyday battle for each of our life's purpose raging. Mom never showed partiality in her love for each of us. She loved us all the same whether we toed the line or not. She passed on this same fairness to all of her grand-children and great-grandchildren. Mom understood the loving impact she could have or not have as a stay-at-home mom. I would say the job description she chose was simple—she would pray hard and love deep—which finally paid huge dividends I am certain she is still enjoying in heaven. In fact, her value of equal love for all her offspring was so strong, each one of us could tease at her funeral that we were her favorite. This was the kind of tongue-in-cheek laughter she left as part of her legacy. Not wanting to repeat the past she had grown up with, Mom de-termined to bridge our family into a new and healthier future marked by both prayer and unconditional love—and that she did.

She didn't spend her entire day in prayer, though. Once she finished praying, she made breakfast for all of us and sent us off to school. She was so involved at the Trumbull school over the span of all of her children's schooling that in 1959 the school's principal issued her a "Certificate of Service" for her twenty-one years of volunteer service. I still have the certificate with all of our names and her "Outstanding Record" inscribed on it. My mother apparently liked this school so well when she went there as a child, she returned later as a volunteer even faith-fully helping to man the voter registration table located in the Trumbull Elementary gymnasium every four years.

Just as Mom had done before us, we all walked to the same elementary school only five blocks from our home at 409 North Pleasant. Mom and Dad took ownership of this house after they married and Grandma Sweet then moved to the farm outside

Battle Creek. The world outside of Jackson affected me personally during my elementary school years because it was the time surrounding World War II. I was about six years old when the war officially started for the United States and ten years old when it ended. None of my relatives were drafted or volunteered in the war, but we had neighbors whose family members did go. Food like tuna fish and energy sources like gasoline were rationed during the war years, so when the war ended I broke my church's dancing prohibition and joined my neighbors to dance for joy in the street when we heard about the men returning home from the war and rationed foods and gasoline becoming freely available again.

We seldom traveled more than a few miles from home because traveling was no small feat for nine people in those days, so when we did travel it had to be really important. What my parents deemed really important was visiting the one and only grandparent left on each side of our family—Grandpa Smith on my dad's side and Grandma Sweet on my mom's side. Both of their spouses had died at a young age, and they chose never to remarry. I never did meet my Grandpa Sweet because Mom, an only child, was only twelve years old when he died, but I did at least meet Grandmother Smith who passed away when I was only two or three years old.

Both grandparents lived on farms. Most frequently we traveled to my paternal grandfather Hobart Smith's house 5 miles away in Munith, Michigan. His religious background was Methodist. Two of his three boys lived close by his farm, which was a good thing because Grandpa Smith raised both beef *and* dairy cows so he needed all the help he could get. Grandmother Smith's passing never did stop my family from working hard in her kitchen the same way she had modeled for us so many years. We even placed glass jars in a huge pot of hot water and canned Grandpa's butchered beef just like she had done. There were no chest freezers or pressure canners, so we had to boil that canned meat several hours to prevent food poisoning. We canned Grandpa's homegrown vegetables, too, after we picked them the same way Grandma had done it. This took so much more time than just going to a grocery store and buying food, but this was one way my parents were able to make ends meet. We got our chicken eggs from one of my uncles, Lawrence Smith, who lived nearby Grandpa's farm. There we visited relatives and picked up groceries. We really did both at the same time!

Over the Kalamazoo River to Grandmother Ella Sweet's house we would rarely go, traveling about 50 miles away from home to just outside Battle Creek, Michigan. Grandma Sweet's farm population included chickens, cattle, and sheep. She also did a lot of canning, but we didn't get a lot of food from her because she lived so far away. Mom allowed my sisters and me plenty of opportunities to help her in the kitchen with cooking and baking since Mom had learned to make the best pie crust ever from Grandma Sweet. I took to homemaking so well, Mom considered me her peer. I enjoyed being given adult status, despite my chronological years being few.

Life was not all work for Grandma Sweet who did not share our family's same set of beliefs. Grandma Sweet was sweet on watching movies at the movie theater. In fact, every Thursday Grandma went to visit her sister in the city where the two of them went out for lunch, followed by a spell at the movie theater, and finished off with some necessary shopping. The few times I broke through my propensity toward homesickness to spend a few summer days at Grandma's house, I remember Grandma sneaking me to the movie theater. I was taught at home and church that if Jesus returned while you were in the movie theater, you would not go to heaven; you would be left behind. It was during these few trips to the movie theater that I learned to fearfully ask God not to come back quite so soon. Grandma Sweet made it her mission to make sure each of us Smith children made it to the movie theater. Much to her chagrin, Mom always somehow found out. This knowledge made Mom angry because she had left behind all of the drinking, smoking, and attending movies.

After my mom and dad married, they took over the house at 409 North Pleasant Street in Jackson while Grandma Sweet moved to the farm in Climax, Michigan, bought and cared for by one of her previous boarders, Robin Clifford, or "Uncle Bob" as we affectionately called him. My oldest brother Ronnie went over to Grandma's farm to help on the weekends during his high school years, and after graduation he moved right in with them. Once Uncle Bob passed away, Ronnie took over the farm. A few years later, Ronnie married MaryEllen Barton and settled there.

Our trips to both grandparents' houses were quite the sight. Back then we did not have a big passenger van or even a mini-van. No, we owned an average Chevy sedan. Imagine all nine of us packed into a sedan designed for six with no air conditioning. Little Dianne would lie across the back shelf of the car, three of us would sit in the back bench seat with two more children on the back seat's floor. Finally, my parents with the one remaining child would sit across the front row bench seat.

> *Imagine all nine of us packed into a sedan designed for six with no air conditioning.*

None of us gave seat-belts a thought because they weren't even available.

One Sunday afternoon my entire family drove westward one hour to our Grandma Sweet's house to pick up my brother Ronnie and to have lunch with Grandma and Uncle Bob. At some point during our visit, Dad realized our car would not make it back home in its present condition, so we borrowed Uncle Bob's two-door coupe. With Dad, Mom, and Dianne in the front seat; Carolyn and Sandy curled up on the back window shelf; and Ronnie, Jerry, Darlene, and me in the trunk, we started out. We made just one stop at a gas station on our return trip home. I distinctly remember the astonished looks from all the onlookers as Dad let the four of us out of the trunk before he bought the gas and let us climb back into the trunk afterward. We all made it home safely. It was difficult for all nine of us to travel together but when we did, we were certainly a close-knit family!

Our home church was Loomis Park Baptist in Jackson, Michigan, where my whole family attended every Sunday and Wednesday night without fail. Dad was a stickler for being punctual for everything including church, which made for a hectic scene every Sunday morning getting us all ready for church on time. It was only made doable by all of the preparation the prior night. Up until about the end of the war, we together enjoyed listening to the adventures of *Sergeant Preston of the Yukon* from our only form of technology—the radio—every Saturday evening before our church preparation routine began. Dad was always the first to be ready on Sunday morning, so he would routinely warm up the car and honk its horn to help hurry us along. This practice worked; we never once arrived late for church. Once there each of us would hurry off to our appointed Sunday school classes before the worship service. In the main service, we consistently sat together near the front of the church. After church all of us always went home to eat Mom's previously prepared meal at our dining room table and, at times when there was a traveling minister at church, the minister came home to squeeze in around the table with us. My mom would not even turn away hosting an entire visiting quartet. She must have exercised supernatural insight to arrange thirteen people around one average size table. I loved Sunday dinners because that was the one and only day of the week we got dessert whether we had guests or not. Mom and Dad shopped for bananas on Saturdays. This was our favorite fruit not available from either grandparent's farm. Mom became an expert at making chocolate cake and different kinds of pies for Sunday dessert. We would savor the sweet, chocolate flavor as we sat around listening to Polish music radiating from our Motorola. Or, we would burn off the dessert calories playing outdoors with all of the many neighborhood children before tidying up to return to church for youth group followed by the Sunday evening service.

Dad served as an elder at Loomis Park Baptist after he and Mom were born again of the Spirit there, becoming the first known generation of Christians in our family. Their spiritual birth came at about the same time as my natural birth. Loomis Baptist was an active church, and my life regularly revolved around church and school. By the time I was in ninth or tenth grade, I transferred from mere membership in the youth group to leadership of the youth group at church. Following in the Southern Baptist tradition, we were not allowed to go to movies, dances, play cards (except Old Maid), or wear make-up. When it was time in my public school gym class to learn square dancing, my mom wrote a letter to my gym teacher asking that I be excused from the dance classes. The school made the accommodation so I could sit out on a bench observing, but not actively participating in the square dancing. I never felt bad about participating in this soft form of protest instead of the dancing because dancing was against not only my religion, but also the religion of all my close friends as well. Despite my friends and my long list of limiting rules, we still had a lot of fun together at home, school, and church. Our church was our extended family.

Because we lived in a family-oriented neighborhood, we had a lot of children to play with and so our street came alive with all kinds of game playing in good weather. Our summer fun also included bicycling to a lake around five miles away and playing various sports like baseball, which I played on a city-wide team. Each geographical section in the city of Jackson had an intramural Kiwanis baseball team. For a good four years, I was on the northern section's girl's team, and we intensely competed against the other teams. It was usually fun, but sometimes my team would be on the verge of getting into fist fights with other team members when our team won. Watching this prefighting taunting sure was nerve-wracking for my mom who was very, very protective.

Even though all of us children spent a significant amount of time playing sports and Dad spent much of his time working, my entire family always somehow carved out time to eat dinner together in the evenings. On one of those occasions, about the time I was fourteen years old, a group of fire trucks flew past our house. Alarmed by the unusual sound of the sirens, we all jumped from the table at the same time and attempted to go out the front door in one big group. The first two or three of my family members got stuck inside the door frame trying to exit, which blocked the rest of us from exiting to witness the excitement outside. Our front door was just wide enough for one person at a time to go in and out, not a whole family of nine! We never needed to pay for comic relief because we created our very own.

When I reached junior high school age, I was ready to walk the farther distance (about a mile) to East Jackson Junior High, so for the next three years I walked to and from this school. When I returned home, my schedule was full just like my siblings' schedules. All seven of us children rotated chores like washing and drying dishes, sweeping, and cleaning up after ourselves until it was time to do homework. Dad made sure we were in bed by around 9:00 p.m. Grades 10, 11, and 12 were housed at Jackson High and, by that time, I could choose between walking or riding the city bus to school, so most often I rode the bus for 10 cents each way unless I had a late game of sports. At East Jackson Junior High and Jackson High School I was involved in all kinds of sports. Baseball, volleyball, and field hockey were my favorites, and I also participated in swimming. Out of the 500 plus students in my grade alone, I had many friends who I played sports with and competed against, but my closest friends before my senior year were those who went to Loomis Baptist.

Although there were many choices to be made in those early years of growing up, probably the choice that had the greatest effect on me was when I was seventeen years old and my mom was invited to visit Pentecostal services held in a small church named Summit Gospel in Vandercook Lake, just outside my hometown of Jackson, Michigan. By 1950 the Latter Rain Movement had spread to Bethesda Missionary Temple near Detroit, Michigan, about 80 miles east of Jackson. The pastor at Summit Gospel had participated in the movement in Detroit before returning to Vandercook Lake. For almost a year, Mom, along with her closest friends, attended the lively services on nights when our family was not committed at our home church,

Loomis Park Baptist. Mom became so excited about the baptism of the Holy Spirit she finally received, she wanted all the rest of her family to experience the same present-day freedom, prophecy, tongue speaking, worship, and supernatural joy. Mom urged me to go along by saying, "DeeDee, you can hardly believe it. It is so wonderful!" When I finally went with Mom as a spectator, I could not help but laugh at first because the scene looked foolish to me, but once Dad led the way, I accepted and received the baptism in the Holy Spirit, too. My entire family began attending many of the Holy Spirit infused revival services, although reluctantly at first, until we all became filled with supernatural signs of the Holy Spirit. I still cannot find words to fully explain it all, but I can say I could feel God's warm presence and see the joyous effect on me and my family. I knew whatever it was, it was genuinely from my good God who I wanted to know better.

My family's Baptist church wanted nothing to do with this move of the Holy Spirit. They firmly believed they already had the baptism of the Holy Spirit at salvation. Speaking in tongues, a part of the Latter Rain Movement, was not a part of being baptized in the Holy Spirit as far as they were concerned. Because my dad was an elder at Loomis Baptist and I was one of the leaders in the youth group, our new relationship with the Pentecostal church complicated our lives. I was so excited about my fuller understanding of the baptism of the Holy Spirit, I desired all my friends in the youth group to know and experience it as well. That led me to, without permission, invite Ernie Norman, the Pentecostal youth leader, to come and speak to the Loomis Baptist youth group. He accepted the invitation, and we had a wonderfully joyous service. This did not go over well with the Baptist church leadership.

My initiative to invite the Pentecostal preacher to my church set in motion events I did not intend or expect at all at the time. I was perfectly content attending both Loomis Park Baptist at the same committed times I always had and filling in other extra times with Summit Gospel attendance. My continued plan was not to be. One Sunday morning, not long after my unrequested invitation of Pentecostal Ernie Norman to our church, our distraught pastor stood up and stated right from the pulpit he had heard that my dad Llewellyn Smith, an elder at Loomis Park Baptist and the head of his home, did not have control over his family and especially his "silly, old woman" of a wife because Dad was attending Pentecostal services with her. Now, the exact words may have been a bit different from what I now recall, but my dad's interpretation of the pastor's words was certain. My dad and his family were walking away from their sterling church membership at Loomis Park Baptist. If the reverend thought this sort of verbal pressure would sway my dad away from attending the Pentecostal church, he was barking up the wrong tree. Realizing our season at the Baptist church was over, my father peacefully led his entire family up and out of our well-worn pew in the first row toward the back and right out the church's main doors that day before the service was over—never to return again. Dad sure did prove he had some kind of "control" over his family that day. It seemed more to me like Moses voluntarily leading his people out of Egypt. This day was the beginning of the hardest and saddest season in my life. I had so many friends at Loomis Baptist, including a boyfriend who was part of the youth group. That youth group was my social center. Our exodus was devastating to me at a time when I was just going into my senior year at Jackson High School. As far as I could see, it was not a good time for any kind of change. After my family's exodus from the Baptist church, my friends from that church had nothing to do with me. I was shunned. Needless to say, my senior year was difficult, painful, and lonely. I doubted I would ever have any friends again. I had "faith" to believe I would never marry. I thought my life was over.

Little did I know that God had another choice for me to make. Until this time, I had really desired to be a hair dresser for a career. My plan was to go to school for cosmetology in Detroit, Michigan, upon high school graduation. Although my major in high school was secretarial and I had a secretarial job at the Jackson Credit Bureau waiting for me the summer after high school, I still wanted really to learn how to do hair. After all, I had years of practice making my younger sisters' hair fashionable, so it seemed reasonable to be further trained and paid for the skill. During high school, I had a wonderful Christian teacher by the name of Adele Erickson for my secretarial courses. She was one of Mom's four Baptist friends who accompanied Mom to the Pentecostal revival services. She was very instrumental in helping me to navigate my senior year, especially learning to walk in obedience to the will of God despite my uncomfortable circumstances.

One Sunday morning, several months after we had ushered ourselves out of the Baptist Church and into membership at Summit Gospel Pentecostal church, two people came from Elim Bible Institute of Lima, New York, to speak. One speaker was Ivan Q. Spencer, the founder of Elim, and the other was his daughter Eva Butler, a missionary from Kenya, East Africa. What a wonderful service we had that day in our new church where Dad once again took on the responsibility of eldership. I made a big decision that particular Sunday, a choice that would forever change the life of a mama's girl from a large, tight-knit family, who never before envisioned herself venturing very far away from home. For me adventures outside of Jackson, Michigan, were only imaginary scenes for the likes of Sergeant Preston. This childlike perception began to shift that day when I made the good decision to attend Elim Bible Institute, the mysterious place of which these two special speakers told. When I first made the decision, I did not realize the distance between the city of Jackson, Michigan, and the tiny town of Lima, New York, was some 400 miles. What a big, long-distance choice I made that day! My world changed forever. The first day of August 1953, I attended Elim Bible Institute.

Dad had stuck with the same company for over three decades even after it relocated from Michigan to Illinois. I had already moved out-of-state when Dad's job moved out-of-state, so I never experienced the time when he spent the weekdays at work in Illinois and only the weekends at home. Mom's work never did move out-of-state because she served faithfully as a stay-at-home mom right in Michigan for as long as I can recall. I viewed both of my parents as very smart and successful, despite the fact that both of them only went to the eleventh grade. Looking back on the first eighteen years of my life, I am grateful God gave me such wonderful parents: parents who left their legacy of loving God and serving people.

REFLECTION QUESTION:

When has your life taken an unexpected turn that turned out better in the long-run?

CHAPTER 7
Life After Loomis Park

Immediately following my high school graduation in 1953, I worked at the Jackson Credit Bureau for the summer. I returned to this job each summer between years at Elim and left each fall to return to Elim Bible Institute in beautiful Upstate New York. Though I had made a firm choice to attend Elim in the fall of 1953, the agony I felt after actually leaving my home, parents, and family was excruciating. My decision became a reality when my parents left me in my dorm room and headed back to Michigan. This time my dad couldn't just drive over and rescue me the way he had two years in a row when I was a child attempting to sleep over at my friend's 4-H summer camps. There were many days, in fact two weeks, when I really questioned the choice I had made. Would I be able to stay or not? I was not sure at the time. I so wanted to be back home with my family. I was so homesick, I could not unpack my suitcase and settle my things for two whole weeks. During this transition time, every time I went down to the dining hall to eat, I would cry. Every time I would cry, Dean of Women Eva Watson Clark would take me into the president's office so President Carlton Spencer and his secretary, June Klotzbach Lindsay, could pray for "little Gloria." This was repeated just about every day for two weeks.

It was on a Saturday, two weeks after my arrival, when my roommate Ruth Little Nugent Marsh told me she would be going out on a ministry assignment that afternoon leaving me alone in the room. That was the first time I was alone in my dorm room. Well, what would I do? Would I be able to stay alone? That afternoon, alone in that dormitory room on 3rd floor east, God met me in a special way. From I Peter 2:9 God made me to know that I had been chosen by Him, to tell others about Him. That was it; I unpacked my suitcase and my life at Elim really began.

Yes, that was the turning point, a decisive choice for me, a no-turning-back choice. I had crossed the Rubicon, and I was moving forward. After a rocky start, three years later in 1956 I graduated. The new, true friends I made at Elim are still my friends today, although several have passed away. They all had an impact that somehow changed my life for the better.

Probably a month or so after the day I decided to stay at Elim while I was cleaning off tables and wiping trays (every student in those days had to put in ten hours of work to help offset tuition), a freshman, one of twin brothers from New York City by the name of Paul Johansson, walked up to me and unsolicitedly said, "Do you know what I think of you? I think you are a flirt!" I just about died when he said that for I was so shy and was just trying to adjust to Elim. Here this guy came up and started his own dialogue about me in front of me! What I later learned was that Paul was friends with Mike Chiapperino, a friend also from New York City, who had just graduated from Elim in 1953. Mike came from the same church Paul was from and after graduation served as the Elim mail collector for the town post office as well as an Elim assistant cook. Since Mike was privy to the postal mail, he noticed I was receiving mail from not one, but two young men! One of the young men was a military friend of mine, and the other guy was one of my friends from my Michigan hometown. There was also a second witness to all of my "flirtatious" mail—a young man at Elim, whom I had met at Bethesda before I went to Elim, who would tell Paul about all the male mail I was receiving from home. So, Paul's way of beginning our courtship was by proclaiming I was a flirt right to my face! I was initially horrified and shocked by his unfair words, but those were the very words that began our relationship and a journey that in looking back over sixty years wonderfully opened the whole world to me.

I am so grateful today that I made the choice, or I should say I allowed God to make it through me, to attend Elim Bible Institute because it began a new way of life for me. It was at Elim during times of outstations, chapel services, classes, and even manual duties that God opened up a world of adventures and challenges for me. My life growing up was more routine. I knew what to expect almost every day. Our family's exodus from Loomis Park marked the beginning of unexpected changes to my life. Adjusting to unplanned changes took time for me. Chapel service times, prayer times, and times quietly waiting on God happened in the setting at Elim where I could hear God speak many things about my life and His good desire for me through all the change. The world looked bigger to me. Growing up in a small American city, living in a large family, involved in a great church, and planning for a career in cosmetology was all I had seen before Elim. Then moving to Elim and meeting Paul Johansson changed my life forever. Or, should I say, meeting Paul Johansson changed my whole family's life forever? One time Paul even remodeled part of my parents' kitchen. It went something like this:

"Why does the door open inward?" Paul inquired. "Everyone sitting at the table has to get up when the door opens."

"That is how it's made," Dad matter-of-factly answered.

"Do you want to change it to open out and make more room?" Paul questioned again.

"I guess so," Dad acquiesced as this new idea settled in.

They loved him even more after he changed the door. It worked so much better swinging out. They thought they couldn't fix the door themselves, but Paul did not forsake his can-do attitude even when it came to my parents' kitchen door.

Besides my own mother and Paul's mother, another woman held a mother's influence in my life at this time. Eva Butler, whom I first met back at my home church in Jackson, provided on-site guidance for me during my Elim stay. As graduation approached, Eva somehow heard I felt called to Africa and provided a profitable answer to my earnest question: "I am not a school teacher or anything like that, so what can I do?" She immediately directed me to hold out my hands as she declared, "Whatever your hands find to do, do it."

After graduating in May 1956, Paul's aunt Jenette Williams and I traveled to Williamsport, Pennsylvania, where that summer we helped George and Ruth Veach pioneer a church. Jenette and I did house-to-house canvasing, children's ministry, and filling in at anything and everything for a short season. After that I returned home and went back to work at the Credit Bureau to prepare for my upcoming marriage to Paul Johansson on November 10, 1956.

We married, went on a Michigan honeymoon, and subsequently drove to Meshoppen, Pennsylvania, where we accepted the senior leadership at a one-year-old church. That church leadership knew about Paul and me because I had gone to Meshoppen, Pennsylvania, for one of my outstation assignments while I was a single student at Elim. I was there just for a weekend of ministry, but it was enough to make a positive connection. The pastor who was ready to leave that church had called Elim and asked if Gloria Smith and her new husband would come and take responsibility for the church there. Although there were other invitations, it didn't take Paul and me long to become convinced this was indeed our first joint assignment. I told Paul I was the door to our first ministry. God taught us so many wonderful lessons of faith in this small church at this one-of-a-kind location.

How God provided for us many times. At times food would be miraculously placed at our back door. Other times, while picking up our mail at the post office, we would discover we were holding a bill in one envelope and the cash to pay the bill in another envelope. Our first year of ministry in Meshoppen, we took no money from the church. We lived strictly by faith. The second year we received one-half the amount of the offering, but it met our needs and God multiplied it. When Paul proposed to me in Jackson back in the summer of 1955, his proposal was, "I may not be able to give you houses and lands, but I can promise you we will do the will of God." The will of God has always been important to me, and Paul's promise has been kept as our journey continues.

If I chose a theme song for my life, I would choose the old-time hymn "Submission," a song that has led me from as long as I can remember. I still enjoy singing to myself the chorus to this hymn:

Not what I wish to be, nor where I wish to go.
For who am I that I should choose my way?
The Lord shall choose for me, 'tis better far I know.
So let Him bid me go or stay.

REFLECTION QUESTION:

*Have you ever made a good decision that headed your life
in a whole new direction?*

Mom & Dad Smith

High School Hockey

Gloria—Michigan

The Smith Clan

Three Smith Generations

Gloria's High School Graduation

Paul, Jenette, Rob and Gloria: EBI 1956

The Smith Family: Ronnie, Carolyn, Jerry, Dianne, Sandy, Gloria, Darlene, Mom & Dad

SECTION III
PAUL & GLORIA

CHAPTER 8
Marriage and Ministry

Gloria voiced just one request for our wedding day. She asked me to make sure my fingernails were free from the black printing ink and grimy car grease she had seen my fingernails covered with many times during our courtship. She shared with me that dirty looking fingernails happened to be one of her pet peeves. Wanting to please my bride and not knowing exactly how I would accomplish her request for our wedding day, that morning I decided to soak my fingers from the tips up to the first knuckle in full strength bleach. The bleach did the job. My fingers had not looked that clean in years. The only problem was as soon as I stood in the front of the church and waited for Gloria to walk up the aisle in all of her radiant beauty on November 10, 1956, I realized I had created a new problem. The aroma of bleach began to fill the air. She later told me as soon as she stood at the altar by my side, she already knew exactly how I had accomplished her request because of the nasty fragrance surrounding us.

My second problem that day came right after the ceremony. With all of the chivalry I could muster, I strode out to our car to start it up so the heater would have time to heat up against the cold November air. Nothing fired when I turned the key. After some inspection under the hood, I, dressed in the finest black, rented tuxedo in Michigan, concluded the generator was shot. I recruited a couple of my similarly dressed wedding attendants to help me underneath the car to remove the useless generator. I found a volunteer to drive me to the nearest shop where I bought a sound generator, which we quickly installed into the Nash to make her ready for Gloria and my honeymoon trip around Lake Michigan.

After our honeymoon, we immediately moved to the small town of Meshoppen, Pennsylvania. My brother Rob was pastoring an Assembly of God church in Waverly, New York, about 45 miles north of where Gloria and I moved. Rob was a single pastor who lived in a 19-foot travel trailer church parsonage. Since we lived so close, Gloria and I visited him often. An added bonus to his company was his ownership of cutting-edge technology. Rob owned an 8-inch portable television set he kept concealed in his traveling parsonage. At that time watching television was among a list of sins in our church circles, along with dancing and card playing; therefore, Rob had to store the rather large television aerial underneath the trailer by day. Then, in the dark of night, he attached the antenna to the trailer's roof so we could watch *The Sid Caesar Show* and *Gunsmoke* on the snowy, black and white screen. We agreed the best name for this television was "Little Lucifer." While it seems silly today, at the time the television was such a new technology no one knew whether it was good, bad, or both; so, it was easier just to evaluate it as purely bad.

Almost one year after we were married, our 5 pound, 9 ounce son Mark Paul was born on October 25, 1957, in a large house nearby converted to serve as the local hospital. That hospital—Tyler Memorial—no longer exists, being replaced by a much larger and more modern one located two miles from the original. Mark forever became a source of great joy to our hearts! Since Mark's birth came a year prior to our Africa support-raising travels, he was at the perfect age to spend some Grandpa and Grandma time with my parents in New York City while Gloria and I traveled together. We have no regrets about leaving Mark in that one stable location and bonding with his paternal grandparents during our short four-month period of fundraising for our first African assignment.

God not only used fundraising to support our time in Africa, but He also once again used an unexpected means: Reverend Parker from Toledo, Ohio, who happened to be a representative for Kitchen Kraft waterless cookware and who collected on our behalf each and every pot and pan available at the time. This thoughtful, generous preacher mailed the entire aluminum set in two large boxes to New York City for us to pack into our cargo on the *Robin Gray*. As newlyweds, Gloria and I had attended a home party for Kitchen Kraft when we first moved to Pennsylvania. Gloria cried all the way home from that party because she knew at that time we were unable to afford even one of those high quality pots and pans. Certainly God knew the desires of our heart; both Gloria and I desired safe and efficient kitchen tools. We held steady in our united desire and waited for His provision that ended up being way better than anything we could have imagined. By the time our final Africa assignment ended, we were able to leave all of those trusty pots and pans to all of our new African friends who are still using them to this day!

January 1958 proved to be pivotal to my faith walk. As I dialogued with the Lord in prayer, I said to God, "I don't have the faith to make going to Africa happen." In response, the words the Apostle Paul wrote to the Galatians came to me: "I live by the faith of the Son of God" (2:10, KJV). The felt presence and gentle voice of the Lord confirmed Paul's words: "Take my faith." From this moment on, in every assignment to follow, I took His faith. This is how I prevailed. This truth became a part of me and enabled me to finish each and every assignment. My faith came up short for the assignments requiring a faith bigger than any I had alone. His faith carried both Gloria and me through every assignment regardless of who said they would help us and didn't or who disliked and rejected us. We were careful to finish our God-given assignments utilizing His faith.

REFLECTION QUESTION:

*When have you needed His faith because your own faith
was too small for your assignment?*

CHAPTER 9

Kenya

One looming obstacle Gloria and I spent considerable time praying about was our lack of money to pay for the passenger tickets for our first voyage to Kenya. We sensed we were to order the tickets before we had the money to pay for them. We did. I thought this step of faith was huge at the time, but really it was just one small step in a line of faith steps. Because faith is a muscle, I knew I must strengthen it through exercise. Choosing Elim, taking our first pastorate in Meshoppen, Pennsylvania, and buying these first tickets to Africa all appeared to me as big steps of faith at the time, but they were actually smaller stepping stones preparing me for future major steps requiring millions of dollars to run faith-based organizations. Only those who see the invisible can do the impossible.

> *Only those who see the invisible can do the impossible.*

Stepping onto the freighter, the Holy Spirit quickened the following thought into my mind: There is a difference between a wilderness and a famine. While crossing the ocean I meditated on the thought and concluded the wilderness is a place God takes you into to make you stronger. The way out is to trust. A famine is because of disobedience, and the way out is repentance. It's quite simple. If you are disobedient, you are in a famine and need to repent. The problem is to the untrained eye they look the same. This lesson kept me through many difficult times.

We finally arrived at the Mombasa, Kenya, port forty-one days after leaving Brooklyn, New York. Gloria had taken Dramamine for sea sickness, but it had made her sleepy the whole time. It was 1:00 p.m. on May 1, 1959, when we stepped foot onto the eastern shore of Kenya. I had already spoken with our seasoned missionary host Reverend Bud Sickler on a ship-to-shore telephone while we were still out at sea, but close enough to land to see the new Oceanic Hotel from where he called. At first sight, Gloria and I thought the beautiful hotel was the missionary's home, but after arriving we quickly learned he was just visiting for our sake. Once we sailed through customs, we had our first taste (but certainly not our last) of Kenya's customary British fish and chips. We also made our first major purchase while in Mombasa—a brand new 1959 Volkswagen Beetle. It looked like life was going to be a breeze for us in Kenya.

Gloria and I had been praying during our itinerating time to have reliable transportation in Kenya since we knew we would be living 175 miles away from the nearest hospital. We never intended or expected our prayer to be answered in the way it was. We paid in full the 1700 US dollars for the car partly from money that came from the death of my cousin Arthur. Arthur was serving in the US Air Force in December of 1958 when he was killed by a drunk driver. His parents Uncle Arthur, Sr., my dad's brother, and Aunt Charity, his wife, gave Gloria and me $500 from the tithe of Arthur's insurance policy, plus an additional $50, so we could buy a reliable car in Kenya. The cost for our new car could not have been more expensive. What a sobering gift we received from my grieving aunt and uncle. Families are important in God's plan for your life.

> *Families are important in God's plan for your life.*

REFLECTION QUESTION:

Who has paid the price for you to get where you needed to go?

CHAPTER 10
Bukuria Mission

In our brand new Volkswagen, I drove Gloria and Mark the 300 miles from Mombasa to Nairobi for the first part of our two-leg journey toward our divinely appointed assignment—Bukuria Mission. We aimed to settle in the capital city of Nairobi eventually; however, in between time, our objective was to make ourselves useful at the rural mission station at Bukuria—another nine hour drive westward past Nairobi on a mostly winding dirt road. It was during our two-day stay in Nairobi that Gloria and I experienced our first extreme culture shock from which we never fully reoriented ourselves. At the comfortable Anglican guesthouse in Nairobi where we spent our first overnight, the woman in charge informed us our eighteen-month-old son would have to eat separately from us since children were not allowed to sit for dinner at the same table as the adults. There was no way either of us was going to allow our son out of our sight in this new country so we separated, taking turns eating with the adults and watching Mark. We left there and hurried on to Bukuria where our time in between Bukuria and Nairobi stretched out over nearly three years before our replacements arrived. We followed senior missionary Bud Sickler to the back country of Bukuria, 15 miles from the Tanzania border. I remember we stopped at one place along the road when Bud stepped out of the vehicle and asked directions. As I watched him talk fluently in Swahili with a Kenya tribesman, I envied his ability to communicate so freely. I knew to really get close to the people, I must speak their language, and right then and there I committed myself to do that.

A rather large house sat amid the 10-acre Bukuria Mission. The acreage included a shop, a primary school, two smaller missionary houses, and a church founded in the 1940s by Roy and Teresa Hill among the Wakuria tribe. Not only would our family settle in this house for a season as soon as our boxes of belongings arrived, but a senior missionary woman named Edith Knoll and her two little adopted African sons would also share the same house as soon as I divided it in two. Before I could start our house's reconstruction into a two-family dwelling, though, I was asked to complete a more urgent construction need at the Suna House some 20 miles away and some 3500 feet above sea level. Wanting to ready our new home as soon as possible for my wife and son, I pushed myself beyond my limits working on the Suna House, which served the nearby Luo tribe. I ended up enduring a two-week stay at a little Catholic hospital located 175 miles away in Kisumu because I was suffering from yellow jaundice. The hospital staff finally released me to finish recovering at home, which proved very useful because while I was recovering at home I was able to use the pine wood from our big home-made shipping crates to build kitchen cupboards and to use the strength God provided to reconstruct our house into the necessary two-family dwelling.

There was no shortage for women's ministry in the back country. I, Gloria, taught Bible courses a couple of times a week at Taranganya, the station's mission school, and I traveled with Eva Butler periodically for women's meetings. I did all of the bookkeeping for the mission station, and I had the distinct privilege of typing the first translation of the book of Mark into the Kuria language. This was because Chacha Omahe, a self-taught Kuria tribesman, together with the British Foreign Bible Society needed my help and the help of my Kuria character typewriter to get the book of Mark into print. When finished it was the first and only book of the Bible in the Kuria language! As if that weren't enough for my assignment list, I also needed to change the water filters every two or three days to provide clean drinking water, to haul other water home for washing, to check our outhouse for bugs, to pour lime into our outdoor "bathroom" as necessary, and to shoulder much more detailed work just to keep the household livable. Truly, I was obeying Eva Butler's motherly advice to do whatever my hands found to do.

———•◦•———

Gloria and I also volunteered to help out the TL Osborn organization during our stay at Bukuria. My job was to set up three rotating monthly area meetings to encourage pioneering pastors who were being supported through funds from the United States. The meetings were designed for teaching the pastors and giving time for them to report how many people were born again, how many were healed, and any other noteworthy happenings. It was Gloria and my added responsibility to take the pastors' rough reports and rewrite them into easy-to-read English before mailing the reports to the funding Osborn organization. What a privilege it was for us to serve the TL Osborn ministry for three years in this way! As with any great learning experience, Gloria and I noticed an area where we thought improvement could be made to the Osborn model. That area was a lack of the building of indigenous churches because all of the churches were dependent on overseas finances. Gloria and I agreed we would establish a deliberate change as we moved forward. Any churches we worked to establish in Nairobi would be self-sustaining.

If Gloria and I were judging this particular assignment by how safe our surroundings appeared to be at the time, we certainly would have determined our surroundings appeared rather unsafe. We arrived at the mission station toward the end of the Mau Mau rebels' amnesty time and toward the beginning of the Congo uprising, which sent refugees into neighboring countries including Kenya. By 1960 the Congo revolt had exploded into a full blown civil war. Some missionaries lost their lives in the war and others lost their homes, some even fleeing through the safety of our little Bukuria Mission station. It was a very dangerous time.

While our ultimate trust rested in God's mighty right hand and His holy arm, we made a decision while visiting Nairobi that proved to be very useful. We adopted a dog that was a cross between an Alsatian and a Boxer. We named him Sarge, and I trained him in willing obedience. He grew into a faithful protector, especially for Mark. I taught Sarge to find Mark. As part of Sarge's training, I would leave Mark in an African hut belonging to a family friend. Then I would go home and command Sarge to go find Mark. Sarge quickly learned to find Mark wherever he was. I also spent ten months carefully training Sarge to protect our home's front door. No one ever came into our house to steal anything because they knew Sarge's ability.

Sarge demonstrated his protective love for his master one day when two pastors came for a visit. I invited the men to sit in the back yard with Sarge at ease nearby. Immediately, I reached out my hand to shake each pastor's hand when one of the two men refused my handshake. I warned in Swahili, *"Mbwa ni kali,"* which means: The dog is very fierce. We visited and prayed for a short time and when the pastors went to leave, the one who refused to shake my hand earlier found Sarge's teeth wrapped around his wrist as soon as he took the too-late initiative to reach out and try to shake my hand.

Sarge even watched out for our safety every time we headed out the back door to the outhouse; Sarge made his rounds first checking for snakes and intruders. If the path was clear, he would allow us to go.

One day I decided to take Gloria, Mark, and Sarge for a picnic lunch out in Maasai territory. I had hoped Mark would get to see some of the many animals roaming the area, but all we saw that day was a group of Maasai tribesmen with spears. As soon as Sarge spotted the unfamiliar men, he ran growling and snarling toward them, which provoked the tribesmen to ready their weapons. I yelled and ran as fast as I could before throwing myself between our beloved watchdog and the warriors. Usually Sarge protected us, but that day I protected Sarge from being speared.

On another occasion, five of us *wazungu* (white people) accepted an invitation to a Maasai *manyatta*, an event where mothers build huts for their boys who are transitioning from childhood into warrior adulthood before the boys are circumcised. By day we watched the Maasai entertain us for the three day event, and by night we slept peacefully out under the stars.

I couldn't always go it alone for visitation. When I took Gloria, Mark, and perhaps a few other friends along, I would just drive all of us in our little Volkswagen out to churches located in remote places where never before an automobile had traveled. On one such occasion, a hidden stone hit the rear, cast aluminum engine knocking off an important bolt and creating a nasty hole in the main oil pan, resulting in a hit-or-miss oil leak. I drove that car with extreme care until I was able to replace it.

Approximately 20 miles from Bukuria Mission was its sister mission, Suna Mission, founded by Eva Butler. At the time my family lived at Bukuria, George and June Lindsay and their daughter Georgia lived in the Suna Mission house where I had worked under its hot roof to build a second apartment. George (who had been in Kenya a number of years before we arrived) and I traveled several times in our VW to northern Tanzania, outside the town of Musoma on Lake Victoria. This area truly was an unreached territory. To get there I navigated across the Serengeti Plains through herds of impalas, zebras, and wildebeests. Some of the impalas even jumped over my little Volkswagen as we pushed our way through the herd. Not only did we need to push through impalas, but we also had to push our way through the black cotton soil, which became a slimy mud when wet. By the time nightfall came, we needed to set up camp to get some rest. After setting up camp at one particular site, George decided it was the perfect time to tell me the story of the lion tracks he discovered outside his tent one morning at this very site.

These trips were very important to our assignment because on these trips George and I, along with our brothers in Tanzania, discovered places to pioneer churches. Today, churches continue to grow from the small seeds we planted by faith in late 1959.

I carefully drove that same leaky VW to Nairobi in 1959 for a six-week crash course in Swahili. I learned the structure of the language during that time in order to speak correctly, and as I expanded my vocabulary, I was able to preach freely.

When we were not busy visiting the twenty or thirty bush churches under our care, we traveled to teach Bible throughout the district and to encourage the newly pioneered churches we had begun in Tanzania. When we weren't busy traveling, we spent our time working at our mission station. Some of my responsibilities at home included mechanical work, electrical work, Kiswahili language studies, carpentry, and building. One specific electric-related job I had included keeping the Lister single-cylinder diesel engine generator running. It provided part-time power for the other three families who by now were also living at the station. It was important to keep the mission operation running smoothly since so many people went there for so many different needs including transportation for pregnant women to the closest clinic. One time as I was driving a woman to the clinic, her baby decided the back seat of my car was the best place to be born, and that is exactly what happened. Can you imagine the mess?

I certainly am thankful Gloria made it to the hospital on time to deliver Marcia; however, I disappointedly missed her delivery in July of 1960. Gloria and I had just gone to the English copper mine's doctor for her prenatal checkup when the doctor said, "The baby will not come for at least another three weeks." Seeing I had plenty of time, I decided it would be a good time to replace our oil-leaky VW with a brand new vehicle so Gloria could not only go to the hospital in style, but also actually make it there. I then drove the day after her prenatal checkup to Nairobi to shop for a new 1960 Volkswagen.

—•—

When Paul left for his 300 mile car shopping journey to Nairobi, I decided to get some work done around the house with the sudden burst of energy I felt. It was exhausting work because we had to fetch water outdoors, which we heated on our wood stove for cleaning our home and ourselves in our indoor bathtub. I went to bed that night when, about 11:00 p.m., I had to use the bath-room. Since we never went outside in the night because we would have had to send the dog out to do his usual round of outhouse inspection first, I was forced to use our chamberpot. Much to my surprise, I witnessed evidence that the boy or girl baby was ready for an appearance now and not on the "due" date of July 15 or 16. I had delivered Mark just two years and nine months prior so I knew the time was soon. This new timing was definitely not a factor that went into the arrangements Paul and I had made be-fore he left for Nairobi. We had planned to drive toward Kisumu in two more weeks to stay with some of our missionary friends who lived near Kisumu until further time to go on for baby de-livery at the nice hospital where Paul had earlier been treated for jaundice. Remember also, Paul had made our house into a two-family dwelling where, by now, single missionary Edith Knoll lived. My first thought after I felt the urgency of my new, early due date was to wake Edith. When I told her what was happen-ing, she decided to walk across the compound in the dark to an-other missionary couple's house to ask the missionary couple there to drive me as far as Suna Mission where Eva Butler could drive me the rest of the way to Kisumu in her car. We had no way of letting Eva know ahead of time we were on our way or in need of her assistance. I could feel the excitement in the air and in my heart as I imagined popping our baby out in the back seat of a car along the bumpy, dirt road in the dark of night. We arrived at Eva's home at the Suna Mission compound around midnight, waking everyone up from all of the commotion. Eva put me in the back seat of her car ready to go by 2:00 a.m. for the 170 plus mile journey on to Kisumu. We arrived in Kisumu just before 9:00 a.m. and just in time for a refreshing drink and small break-fast stop at a local hotel before it closed until lunch time. Next, we made our way to the little hospital. I spent from 9:30 a.m. to 2:30 p.m. suffering through the steady contractions before our lit-tle 6 pound, 4 ounce Marcia Kay was born on July 2, two weeks ahead of schedule. Paul wasn't the only person unavailable for the delivery; my doctor wasn't able to make it to the hospital either, but a midwife and the Holy Spirit were there for support.

In those days, women stayed in the hospital for about a week and a half after delivering a baby, which I did. The hospital sent me home assuming I would continue to nurse my second child the way they assumed I had nursed my first. The big problem was I had never nursed Mark. Try as I did, both Marcia and I became very ill in a matter of a few days. Paul quickly drove to our "obstetrician" at the copper mine who advised another hospital visit. We drove all the 170 plus, long miles back to Kisumu for an initial diagnosis of malaria. What I really had was mastitis, which took a full week to heal; at the same time Marcia was hospitalized for two weeks before she recovered from thrush mouth. We took Mark with us this time because we knew it would be too traumatizing for him to wake up again with his mommy off to a faraway hospital.

Two and a half days after I left home to go to Nairobi, I received a telegram from Eva Butler informing me Gloria had delivered a baby girl. Much to my surprise, I learned that the very night after I left, Gloria began to feel labor pains. She immediately made the 20 mile trip to the home of Eva Butler, our senior missionary friend, who drove her the second part of the 175 mile journey to the nearest hospital in Kisumu. Through the night Eva drove over the bumpy dirt roads until they safely arrived at the hospital a bit after 8:30 in the morning. Better late than never is not always true. Late was definitely not better for me when Marcia was born, since I was unable to make it back home until Marcia was four days old. (Incidentally, Marcia was born in Kisumu, less than 40 miles from the birthplace of the father of Barack Obama, the United States' 44th president.)

Gloria always was a trooper even when deep feelings of trepidation dogged her. Her duties at Bukuria Mission included cooking on a wood stove, keeping the kerosene fridge clean and operational, collecting rain water in big tanks on the roof during rainy season, and washing all of the fruit and vegetables we ate (just to name a few of her household tasks). She performed these duties without complaint all during her pregnancy and afterward, even while caring for our two young children in a new culture.

The mission purchased a 350 Triumph motorcycle I used to do church visitation so I did not always have to use our new car. Since the bike was small yet powerful, I used it to get to churches accessible only by a narrow, dirt trail. We also owned a second, smaller 250 Triumph we shared with the Kenyan overseers to enable them to do visitation over a larger territory, too. One of the churches under my care was located in Area B near the Tanzania border and in the Maasai grazing land. To get to Area B, I had to drive the Triumph over a little, low bridge only during the dry season when the water was low. There were a lot of animals in Area B because the British had decided years prior to stop the elephants from crossing from Maasai country into Bukuria tribe territory. The elephants had been stomping out the vegetables grown for essential food. So, the British set up work teams to dig a 5-mile long, by 6-foot deep, by 5-foot wide trench to stop the elephant traffic. I had to drive my little Triumph down the trail that paralleled the trench. The trench had filled up with overgrown bushes over the years, so if trail travelers did not know about the trench ahead of time, they could not see it. The government installed cement bridges across the trench to connect the tribes, but the bridges were designed with about three or four feet worth of four-inch horizontal pipes placed about four inches apart and close to the Maasai side because elephants will not walk across these pipes. One day after a church visit on the Maasai side of the trench, I dropped off a passenger just before I came upon a fallen tree across my trail track. I quickly turned the motorcycle wheel just a wee bit but enough to catch the heavy mud. I was instantly flipped up into the air and down into the trench. By the grace of God, a tree on the inside of the trench caught my ankle so I was hanging upside down from the inside of the trench when I awoke. I saw my motorcycle resting below my head half in and half out of the ditch. I wasn't sure how long

I had been knocked out, but I did know I needed to get my head off of the exhaust pipe quickly before the damage to my head worsened. The hot exhaust pipe had burned a trail right across the top of my forehead. In order to free myself, I had to pull my foot out of my lodged boot and my arm out of my tangled jacket, which made me fall into the bottom of the jungle-like ditch. I was able to climb out of the ditch, but I was unable to dislodge my bike. I found two women nearby who agreed to help me pull the motorcycle out of the ditch. It took the three of us to finally pull the wrecked bike up and out and back onto the trail where the beleaguered bike only started after we pushed it and tapped it into second gear. I drove home knowing I had been saved by my Savior from certain death and perhaps an attack by a wild animal had I not gotten out of the ditch. Since the nearest hospital was 175 miles away in Kisumu, I really did not want to make another trip there; so, I treated my head wound with some of baby Marcia's petroleum jelly. It worked.

Transportation empowers. Not wanting to be the only one with a means of transportation to distant destinations during our time at Burkuria, we had the privilege of overseeing the purchase of many new bicycles for our affiliated pastors to use. These pastors were then empowered to oversee two or three more churches. Pastor John Vick of the Rock Church in New York City became a part of this commissioning exercise by funding these bicycles.

———— • ◦ • ————

Part of my motherly care for our children in our new, adopted culture involved treating worms in our children's butts and stomachs, as well as treating the results of fire ant bites on their legs, torsos, and arms. I never learned any of these nursing skills back in the United States, but here I had to be a quick learner. Also, I quickly learned how to iron with a flat iron heated on a wood stove. I used this heated iron to kill the fly larvae out of all the laundry, including wash cloths and sheets. If I missed any larvae in the ironing, I learned how to pop the little critters out of our skin by painfully pinching them out. I also tried never to miss noticing any little snakes inside the house and big snakes outside so we could avoid them.

Because the local people did not have refrigeration, it was their custom to kill one cow each week. Many times we watched as a skinny cow passed our mission station on its last earthly trip. This was the perfect time to shop for meat because we could buy fresh beef for just 14 cents per pound. We would buy a big chunk of meat (sometimes with dirt and gravel attached), carry it home, wash it off, and cut it up into various butcher cuts like steaks, stew meats, and pieces for grinding (through a hand grinder) into hamburger. Each kind of cut had to be cooked in a pressure cooker to make the otherwise tough meat easier to chew. We were able to spread out eating our meat over a whole week's time since we owned a kerosene powered refrigerator. Any scrap meats were boiled up for Sarge. He was as happy as we were when we fed him this special cooked-in-meat-juice meat mixed with cornmeal!

As if pinching out larvae, hand-grinding tough meat, and producing our own dog food weren't enough, I also got to grind our own homemade peanut butter using the same grinder as I used on the meat. The closest grocery store was some 70 miles away, so it wasn't like we could just run to the store whenever we needed something; we just made it ourselves at home.

With all of the exertion of chores such as this, I needed to create some connections with my home culture and relaxation time. That is one reason why we visited our good friends Dave and Mary Clark who lived just north of Kisumu, some 200 miles from us. On the way to their house we always stopped in Kisumu to buy ice to make homemade ice cream. The Clarks owned one of those hand crank ice cream makers that produced for us a nice sweet treat along with sweet memories. We added to those sweet memories with the Clarks as we spent a number of great vacations together at the beach in Mombasa on the Indian Ocean. One additional sweet treat we enjoyed there was the fresh lobster we purchased from the fishermen at just 14 cents per pound! This began a love for lobster in our children that they carry in their palates even to this day. Fresh, low-cost lobster was just one of the advantages we enjoyed because of living in Kenya.

———•••———

Finally, the anticipated time for us to move on to Nairobi arrived when two missionary couples moved to the Bukuria Mission station. Art Lease, the man who came to replace me, drove in with a nice, roomy station wagon. That was a good thing because our one-year-old Volkswagen Beetle was not big enough for our family of four and all of our earthly belongings; however, our car and Art's station wagon were plenty big enough even with a load of long planks atop. We needed those planks for the makeshift bridges we had to lay over the muddy sections of the road. As soon as our replacement couples had arrived, a two-week long rain had arrived at the same time. We patiently waited for the flooded roads to reopen. We did not want to join the animals that misjudged the power of the flood waters and found themselves swept down the river that normally brought them life-giving water to drink. As soon as the roads reopened, we set out. The first 20 miles of our journey took us three hours. The rest of the trip went much faster as the road became more and more solid.

I have such warm memories of our time at Bukuria Mission station not only because it included the time when our daughter was born, but also because of the wonderful, caring, and hospitable Wakuria people who lived in the area. Life on the Bukuria Mission was peaceful. It was the time we first met my close friend Chacha Omahe. It was a time when we could learn the language. It was a time when true friendships with other missionaries and pastors were developed. It was a time to solidify our indigenous principles. It was a time of faith.

REFLECTION QUESTION:

Do you remember a time when you had to wait patiently before moving forward?

CHAPTER 11
Nairobi or Bust!

We first moved to Nairobi in 1961, two years before Kenya's independence. We temporarily settled into an old British house. We could not settle too deeply into our new home because the owner had it up for sale. Although the British still had political control, their control was showing signs of fading out. Many tribal and political battles were being fought. Two national political parties vied for governmental control. Nairobi's 500,000 population doubled every morning and returned to normal every evening as commuters traveled in and out of the bustling metropolis. Finally, in December of 1963 the Kenya African National Union (KANU) politician Jomo Kenyatta won the election over the Kenya African Democratic Union's (KADU) Ronald Ngala. Kenyatta was a great first president who gave stability to the country despite unproven accusations of leading the Mau Mau rebellion.

All of the city's tension, however, was not the topic of what I believed to be my first order of business for me personally when we arrived in Nairobi. The words of Saint Paul when he arrived in Corinth came to me: "I have many people in this city" (Acts 18:10b). I desired to know who these people were, so Gloria and I sent out preachers into the streets some twenty-five times a week. In fact, three or four of those times I preached while Gloria accompanied me playing her accordion right through the political unrest. One time a rioter assailed Gloria on her head with a dried corncob while she sat on her accordion case playing her instrument. When she first spotted this particular man in the crowd, she knew in her spirit he meant her harm. This caused her to wisely face the ground before he bopped her on her head with the corny cylinder and then walked away. Another time an overzealous man moved out of a mob and got close enough to ruffle up Gloria's hair. These incidents, however, were not enough to ruffle up Gloria's resolve to continue leading worship despite any fears she had to push away; what they also did was to teach her to surround herself with praying believers for insulation from danger so she could keep right on playing her accordion undisturbed while I or a new national believer preached. The prayers, without any police, covered us. The result was what we had our eye on—"many people" were saved through faith in Jesus Christ. Political factions will always fight while the Gospel continues to be preached, resulting in many precious people being added into God's eternal kingdom.

Our first official assignment in Nairobi was at an all-white South African church pioneered by white South Africa's Reverend Nelson. This church gave us some financial support, which we took to invest into the indigenous national work developing out of our weekly and Sunday afternoon street meetings. I would drive the local preachers in our Kombi Volkswagen to various locations in the city, drop them off, and start the street meeting, and they would carry on with singing and preaching. I actually began this practice by myself just once a month on the streets of Nairobi while we still lived in Bukuria, a 300-mile commute away. Now, I had a whole group of preachers and when we finished preaching, we would all sing as we walked back to our base, a 100 by 70 foot warehouse on Duke Street, downtown Nairobi, followed by a flock of people all ready for the Sunday evening service. This was more than religion. Hundreds of these salvations were dramatic as people moved out of darkness and into the glorious light and life of Jesus Christ right in front of mosques and temples. While Gloria and I pastored the nearly eighty South African believers away from the city center, we parallel pioneered a local city church through street evangelization, which eventually developed into All Nations Gospel Church in downtown Nairobi, a name given to it by me and Art Dodzweit when we were in Nairobi for the first few months. All Nations truly was a church of *all* nations. While other full Gospel churches existed in Kenya separately speaking only English or a tribal language, All Nations Gospel Church was the first multi-language, Pentecostal church in Nairobi. We also intentionally established this church without systematic financial support coming from the United States, which was one of the essential principles we had learned from Reverend Elmer Frink during our time at Elim. Frink had introduced us to a book authored by Roland Allen and titled *Missionary Methods: St. Paul's or Ours?* We weren't able to carry the actual textbook to Africa, but we did carry its methods in our hearts and minds; those methods we put into practice. We cannot thank God enough for the privilege of helping to lay a firm foundation for this group of strong believers based out of our helpful Elim training.

The transformation of the Duke Street warehouse into a house of worship started out quite simply. If Art and May Dodzweit and Gloria and I were going to continue to use this corrugated iron building for a gathering of new believers, we at least had to develop it into more than a bare-bones' structure. That is when we put in a concrete floor, painted the building, installed electricity and toilets, and built 16-foot long camphor benches to function as pews. Remember, my brother Rob and I had learned early on that building could be a form of recreation because it was so creative. We were always building something. Rob wasn't there with a made-to-order construction team in Nairobi, but Art Dodzweit and I flowed together well, so we designed and bolted together enough benches to seat two-hundred, fifty people. Working together we accomplished a big project in a short amount of time. Art and his wife May arrived in Nairobi a year before Gloria and I arrived. Now we were working together with the locals to make this brand new church fully functional by the beginning of 1962.

Paul and I led church services plus street meetings every Sunday—one service in the morning at the all South African white church, another at the downtown Kenyan remodeled Duke

Street warehouse church with Sunday school in the morning, two or three afternoon street meetings, and a service again in the evening at Duke Street. Two of the five services were in English and three were in Swahili. During the week we held more street meetings, midweek services at the church, plus women's meetings. By this time Paul spoke fluent Swahili so there was no need for a translator when Paul preached. Also, with all of the women's life skills and Bible fluency meetings I taught all over the city, I had no need to enroll in any language school. At one particular women's meeting just outside the city limit, I was teaching women in the Luo home of one of our church elders. Now their home was a two-room apartment comprised of a kitchen and a bedroom. I was sitting on their bed teaching and trying to be really spiritual when a nauseating aroma crept into my nostrils and down into my stomach. The odor was so strong I could not continue speaking. I notified my gracious hostess of my "problem," and she proceeded to look for the source of my digestive discomfort. Underneath the bed I was sitting on, my hostess pulled out a large crate full of sun-dried fish she had been keeping for a nice boiled fish dinner served with corn meal or rice. I had eaten that delicious meal before, but never before had I sat atop an entire crate of odiferous dried fish. Once my hostess moved the crate full of fish outdoors, I was able to carry on with the Bible study.

I continued to practice my bookkeeping skills I had honed at the Bukuria mission station while in Nairobi serving Elim Fellowship, All Nations Gospel Church, and the Nairobi Pentecostal Bible College all at the same time. Bookkeeping skills were quite different then than they are today. Since we did not have computers, I kept all double-entry records by hand on real paper with a real pencil. It was a very time-consuming process. It seemed as though the duties my hands found to do were as numerous as the grains of sand filling the Seychelles' beaches. I just kept doing whatever my hands found to do, including baking and decorating wedding cakes for the many weddings held at All Nations or even in our home; playing the piano for all of the indoor church services; playing the accordion for the street services; as well as leading women's meetings and Sunday school classes. On top of everything else, it was our responsibility to host all of the guests who came into Nairobi while keeping up with caring for our own family. Hosting included taking the visitors shopping. I had to make arrangements for the steady stream of guests to stay at our house. Most were overseas ministers and leaders holding pastors' seminars in Nairobi. Whatever was requested of me, I found a way enthusiastically to do it with all of my heart as unto the Lord and to bless the people.

Speaking fluent Swahili made it easy for us to set up an evangelistic crusade late in 1962. Art and I, Paul, scheduled an evangelist from the United States and rented a stadium for two weeks. The first night the crusade drew 5000 hungry hearts after our crusade team handed out handbills and did every-

> *Every city has its key to evangelism.*

thing else we could think of to advertise. The second night drew only 4000 people until within five days the crusade had dwindled down to just 500 people in the Donholm Stadium. The American evangelists thought they should move the crusade for a better impact. I told them we couldn't because we had a two-week signed contract for the stadium. I countered, offering to replace the main evangelist. They agreed; I preached. Many souls committed their lives to Christ then; however, because I lived there I saw that no souls were added to the local church. How could people possibly grow into maturity, develop their gifts, and benefit the kingdom unless they were plugged into a local church? To my knowledge, no disciples whatsoever came out of this crusade. Nothing but a lesson learned really resulted from the great efforts put into this big splash of a crusade. So, I prayed asking

God for the key to Nairobi in particular. Every city has its key to evangelism. I believe the Holy Spirit showed me it is "By the foolishness of preaching" (1 Cor. 1:21). The key to Nairobi was the foolishness of preaching wherever and whenever, not a great crusade in one grand stadium at a specific time. Rather than calling people to come to a stadium, I knew I must now continue to send many believers out of the church and into the streets because it wasn't about the means; it was about the message. And this is how the Nairobi warehouse church grew.

The street meetings produced two beneficial results. First, the street meetings provided opportunities for new leaders to develop their preaching skills as they preached the Good News. Second, they provided a means for many brand new Christians to testify of their new found faith. It was these key street meetings that added to the church and birthed the healthy Sunday school ministry.

We also hosted training seminars through the warehouse church. Rev. Winston Mattsson-Boze, a pastor from the United States, traveled several times to Kenya for the express purpose of holding outdoor training seminars in Kenya. I was assigned the responsibility of setting up the seminars for Pastor Bose just as I had done for Oral Roberts and his seminars. In one of these seminars, I was introduced to a man by the name of Samuel Mwatha Kangethe who had been trained at a Baptist Bible school and who was hungry for knowing more of God. He asked if he and his wife Mary could work alongside us. What was different about his request was he did not ask for money as others had who asked to work alongside us. Gloria and I had agreed early on in our ministry in Nairobi we would find ways for people to support themselves so that if we had to leave, their work would continue without our help. We were glad to grant this couple's request seeing them as the possible answer to Gloria's and my earlier prayers for a Kenyan pastor to train to take over and lead the work.

Together we fellowshipped on Sunday mornings, led Sunday school, and held evening services inside the rented and renovated warehouse. In one of the evening services, I saw a commotion in the congregation while I was praying for people in the front of the church to receive Jesus Christ as their personal Savior. There were about 100 people in the service that night, so I couldn't easily get to the commotion in the middle of my prayer. However, Pastor Samuel Mwatha could and did. He slowly and calmly walked over to the commotion and within a minute led the two arguing men into hugging. I was amazed. The next day I asked Samuel what he did and how he did it. He explained to me the following story:

> I walked over to a commotion, listened, and learned there was a large statured man who had lent a small statured man named Zephaniah 10 shillings [equivalent to about $1.50 in the US at that time]. The small man had promised to pay back the sum by the end of the month, which did not happen. When the large man saw the small man at our evening service, he grabbed the little man by the collar and demanded he repay what he owed. The problem was the little man had absolutely no money. So, I solved the problem by reaching into my own pocket and pulling out the small sum. I gave the 10 shillings to the large man and proclaimed, 'He no longer owes you any money.' I turned to the small man and said, 'You don't owe him anymore, so there's only one thing left to do and that is to love one another.'

After listening to Samuel's account, I knew we had the pastor we had been praying for in the making. His heart was right. He was a man of integrity. He was a man of compassion. He was a true pastor. He became my greatest, truest friend! We ministered together for years as All Nations Gospel Church (ANGC) PEFA grew to thousands of members. Out of the "bowels of compassion" (1 Jn. 3:17, KJV) we helped people in dire need, refusing to make them dependent on any of us through systematic foreign support. We did not want to become the center of provision; we wanted God alone to be their center. Samuel and I worked together in order that I never received any credit for even my compassionate giving in accordance with Jesus' teaching that our giving should be done in secret.

Samuel's wife Mary and my wife also ministered effectively together to the women. By the time Gloria and I returned to the USA, there already were five or six churches in Nairobi born out of All Nations and another fifteen or sixteen more out in the surrounding countryside. Samuel faithfully stayed and served in the original Nairobi church until his retirement in 2000 when he found a reliable replacement. Simultaneous to pastoring ANGC, he served as president of the Pentecostal Evangelistic Fellowship of Africa (PEFA), overseeing some 3000 churches. Only God in eternity knows how to judge the extent of this sweet, humble man's contribution to the body of Christ. Truly Samuel was a man who really loved God and people. All Nations Gospel Church PEFA now consists of about 100 churches in the greater Nairobi area alone with hundreds upon hundreds of large churches in the Nairobi Central District of Kenya built in the same design as the first church where I oversaw the building project. Chacha, Samuel, Mary, Gloria, I and others were the original team members who worked well together to see the kingdom established in the central province of Nairobi, Kenya.

As I mentioned earlier describing our time at the Bukuria Mission station, the 1960 slaughter of the Congo uprising sent missionaries and nationals running for their lives and into the relative safety of Kenya. As a result of that uprising, by late 1962 or early 1963 the senior missionary leaders in Kenya realized the handwriting on the wall—Foreign missionaries will not always be in charge. Thus, the missionary leaders called a meeting to be held at a Salvation Army compound on Quarry Road in Nairobi to discuss the formation of an organization that would be fully Kenyan. The special meeting included Bud Sickler, Art Dodzweit, Dave Clark, me, and elders from the work in Mombasa, along with faithful Kenyan leaders from the coast and South Nyanza. I believe there were approximately twenty-five

African leaders in attendance. A chalkboard was set up for brain-storming questions to be written out: Should we call it an evangelistic organization? Shall we name it a fellowship? What shall we call it? Finally, the brethren decided to choose four out of all the words written on the board and put them together into one title that stuck: Pentecostal Evangelistic Fellowship of Africa. That is how the name was born and the acronym PEFA came to be. From here on I became a part of setting PEFA up, making sure that the national Kenyan brethren would accept responsibility for its continuation on their own shilling and initiative.

The chosen PEFA overseer for Taranganya in the Bukuria mission area became Joseph Muhingra, a great man of God. Before I returned to the United States I visited with Muhingra.

I said, "You know, when I first came here all of these Kenyan pastors were knocking on my door asking for help, but God has helped us to put the burden of leadership on their own shoulders."

Muhingra replied, "Yes, that's okay. Now they knock on my door." I had painfully transferred the focus of leadership from myself to the African overseer; however, the immature desire for dependency on other people still had to be worked out in the believers.

As part of seeing God's kingdom established, Gloria and I made a deliberate change as we had agreed upon during our time at Bukuria—All churches we would have a hand in establishing in Nairobi would be self-sustaining. In order to accomplish this, we resolved to allow pastors to join us only very carefully. On one occasion, a pastor came to me in Nairobi asking to join our team. I called together the elders I had trained to meet with this pastor. The elders quickly concluded God had sent him. I replied that I needed to go on record that I believed God did not send him; in fact, I discerned he was only concerned about the money, however, because the elders wanted to go ahead and we worked as a team, I went along with their decision. We went ahead and placed this man into a church on the edge of Nairobi. After just a few months, the man came to *me* asking for more money! I referred him back to the elders who hired him. (Unbeknownst to him, I was already sending money to the church he was "serving" in to help underwrite his current salary.) The elders supported his request by giving him more money and after another few months, he returned asking for more money. This time the elders responded by calling a team meeting to discuss his spiraling requests and, lo and behold, the same elders who at first thought this man was sent from God unanimously decided it was time for him to go. Who did they decide should tell the man of our united decision? Me. So, I did as they wanted and, in a meeting with all the elders present, I informed this man it was time for him to go. Immediately, the man looked at each elder to confirm my directive and each elder shook his head in approval. What a wonderful lesson the elders had learned. After this experience, whenever a pastor or evangelist came not only asking to join us, but also asking for a bicycle, money for their children's school fees, as well as a salary, we told them no. Furthermore, we told them that in Nairobi we don't do it that way. We grow by the effort of the people. We raise up strong, indigenous churches because the people are strong.

On December 15, 1963, Gloria and I had the privilege of attending Kenya's independence ceremonies held in an open stadium built specifically for the occasion and providing enough room to seat 250,000 people. Not knowing whether or not the country would remain stable, many foreigners had left by this time. We had already thrived through many hardships testifying to the fact that Gloria and I were happy and fearless to stand together with all the wonderful people of Kenya and to face whatever else the future brought, for we knew who really held the future.

One important lesson we had learned right away was that people have to change their thinking when moving into a new culture. Coming from the United States, Gloria and I thought it best for people to do things bigger, better, and faster. That was the American way; however, we changed our thinking quickly in Kenya when we adopted their new-to-us way of thinking that people are more important than projects. Our new motto became "Don't ask me about business before you ask me about how I am." In fact, we learned the Swahili greeting *"Habari, hujambo?"* which translates: Hello, is there any bad news? The answer is always *"Si jambo lakini,"* which means: There is no bad news except . . . . It may have been the terrible news was that their mother was dying or their child was very sick. Once you heard the *lakini,* you were then qualified to do business if it did not take away from whatever concerning news they were pondering. This interaction took time. We had to learn to move slowly. We learned that relationships are most important. In fact, they are more important than issues, more important than projects, and more important than getting anything done. This way of thinking helped us to become more caring. It was the best gift they gave us. The best gift a mission worker can receive is a national who loves them enough to tell them the truth. We were gifted with people who would tell us when we were right and when we were wrong. We were free. In fact, Gloria and I appreciated our national brothers so much we helped them before they traveled to other nations like the United States or Rhodesia by providing advice about how to dress. We even helped them shop for clothes that would be considered culturally presentable in whichever country to which they were going. It wasn't us and them. It was we together identifying potential problems, solving them and, thereby, eliminating a lot of talk behind people's backs. Our national brothers loved me enough to share with me the cultural acceptance of male friends holding hands. I was slow to accept this new and different cultural more, but I finally did accept it because I understood it was a sign of connection. I had to get on their wavelength to make us one together.

In December 1963 when Kenya finally obtained its independence, all South Africa expatriates lost their visas. One by one they had to leave. Shortly after we arrived in Nairobi most South Africans had returned to South Africa and Kenya was undergoing "Kenyanization," the movement toward local, national leadership. During this time we met Jenny, a beautiful young woman, who was supporting herself. Jenny agreed to immigrate to the

United States and, with the sponsorship of my parents, relocated straight to Elim for training. While at Elim, Jenny met and married her husband John and together they ended up spending most of their married years ministering back in Kenya where they raised their three children. What a lovely lady we have had the privilege of knowing and loving. Jenny and her husband John worked in Kenya, Rwanda, and Sudan building many churches, which still flourish today.

Art and May Dodzweit realized they also were to move out of Kenya shortly after we arrived in Nairobi. They saw the need in Kampala, Uganda, leaving Gloria and me to carry on, applying the principles we had learned over the past three years while living in Kenya. Later, the benches Art and I had crafted together were disassembled for shipment over to the new Elim church in Kampala. Our first assignment in Kenya was marked by a political transition from a place of foreign rule to a place of national rule and by a transition for many individuals from a place of worldly rule to a place of God's kingdom rule.

During our first assignment on the field, our family spent a special holiday exploring Murchison Falls, the source of the Nile River, located in northern Uganda. By day we breathed in the beauty of the high waterfall as it emptied into the river below filled with hippos and crocodiles. By night we camped peacefully in our tent right along the river sourced out of Lake Victoria. Peace reigned in our hearts as we pondered how much we had come to understand and love this place and its people. We now spoke the same language. Our children had become color blind to skin tones. We had been accepted as family during our five-and-a-half-year, uninterrupted settlement into the African continent and culture before our first furlough.

Our flight back to the United States took us through Egypt's pyramids and onto Israel where we spent a few extra days enjoying the culture and visiting the sacred places of Jesus' earthly pilgrimage. Gloria, the children, and I were able to rent a taxi in Israel to travel across the no-man's land in Jerusalem into the Palestinian territory. We went on from there to Switzerland and

Germany, even visiting both sides of the communist wall, before flying home. Our children always went right along with us as we have always been in it together.

REFLECTION QUESTION:

What long-term service have you given to God?

CHAPTER 12

Itinerary

It was nice to get back to the USA and the rest of the family in 1964. The family dynamics had changed while Paul and I were away those five-and-a-half years with both Paul's grandmother and my grandmother passing away. In those days a person didn't just hop on a jet and fly from continent to continent to attend important funerals or any other important events for that matter. Paul and I missed his brother Rob's wedding and both of our families missed Marcia's birth and growth milestones for the first four years of her life since she was born in Kenya in July of 1960, and we didn't get back to Jackson, Michigan, until July of 1964. That also meant both of our extended families sadly missed witnessing several of Mark's developmental years.

Paul and I jam-packed our one year back in the States with both family time and support raising time. In order to squeeze the most out of this dual duty, I focused on family while Paul focused on support raising.

Paul needed a car to drive around revisiting the churches who had supported us during our first assignment to Kenya. Seeing the need for a car ahead of time, Mark had asked on our way back from Africa what kind of car we would be getting. A perceptive question asked by our six-and-a-half year old son and answered after Paul prayed and received a specific answer to Mark's curious question—a Chevy station wagon. Meanwhile, Paul's brother Robert was serving as an assistant pastor at a church in Rochester, New York. After our arrival in Michigan, a gentleman from the church in Rochester told Paul's brother he felt like the Lord wanted him to give his car to a Johansson. Rob informed the man that he had no need of a car because he had just ordered a new car from Germany. Not being easily dissuaded, the man replied, "If there is any Johansson who needs a car, let me know." With that reply, Rob immediately thought of his twin brother Johansson who needed a car for his time in the United States. Our family gladly received that 1962 Chevy Impala station wagon! It served us well for the 32,000 miles he traveled around several northeastern states raising and maintaining support during this furlough. After Paul was finished with the vehicle, he passed it on to the original owner's daughter and her husband who were just entering the ministry. Certainly God has provision in hand for us if we just wait for His timing.

We stayed with my mom and dad in Jackson, Michigan, which allowed Mark the privilege of completing the second grade at the same school my mother, all my siblings, and I had attended—Trumbull Elementary. Mark experienced my family's love for routine that year. Each and every day his lunch was the same menu: a peanut butter and jelly

> *Certainly God has provision in hand for us if we just wait for His timing.*

sandwich. One day when he didn't see any peanut butter in the house he walked three doors down to ask the friendly neighbor lady if she would make him a peanut butter and jelly sandwich because his grandmother didn't have any peanut butter. Where there's a will, there's a way.

While Paul was away traveling in his station wagon and Mark was away at school, I spent days at home with Marcia and Mom. Some days I even finished personal paperwork upstairs while Mom watched soap operas and Marcia enjoyed the shows' TV advertisements. This was when Mom and Marcia practiced taking turns; Mom watched the soap operas while Marcia talked, then Marcia watched the commercials while Mom talked.

Mark and Marcia experienced their very first winter that year in Michigan. They enjoyed ice skating wearing the little elastic-strapped blades we bought them that fitted tautly around their insulated boots. They looked so cute and confident skating on the same Loomis Park ice rink where I had skated not so awfully long ago. They loved the cold, Michigan outdoors that year when they could skate or sled or throw snowballs for the very first time.

Paul spent January 1965 back home at Dad and Mom Smith's home with us. It was then he built my mom custom kitchen cabinets with a whole new countertop to replace the same old stuff left there by the previous owners. Remember, Mom wasn't one to initiate change. Paul also took the opportunity that January to fill in for Mom's pastor Reverend Herbert Taylor who was convalescing from a lung operation. Since Paul and I were together for this month, we seized the opportunity to evaluate whether or not we should return to Kenya for a second time. We came to an agreement that our work in Kenya was not finished; we had another divine assignment to return to Nairobi, so we began taking steps in that direction.

Once Mark finished the second grade, the children and I were free to travel around with Paul. We made New York City our new home base for the summer to give the children time to get to know Paul's mom, dad, and Gramps. Gramps did not pass away until the year after we spent that summer with him and by then we were back in Kenya. We felt bad because of the changing family dynamics we had missed while we were away in Kenya, but we did what we could to stay as connected as best we could at that time without any DVDs, FaceTime, or mobile phones. We did ship a calabus monkey rug to Paul's brother Rob and his bride Jan for their wedding that we missed during our first assignment in Kenya. They never would have received such an unusual wedding gift if it weren't for our stay in Kenya! Despite our tugging emotions, we accepted the sacrifices we needed to make in order to fulfill our personal God-ordained destinies. We dug a deep well with God so no matter where we were, what we missed, or how long we stayed, we always flourished.

I, Paul, remember vividly coming home and seeing my brother for the first time in five-and-a-half years. The joy in my heart at seeing him exploded into my face and out through my hug. We had always tried to stay connected because we were very close in heart. My brother and I had to be separated but not divided because of our different assignments. This was not easy for either of us. We so wanted to spend as much time as possible together while we had this chance, so Rob, Jan, Gloria, and I enjoyed the 1964 World's Fair in New York City together. Next, we planned a family trip to Florida. It wasn't so much the destinations that brought us so much joy, it was more the time spent together. My brother even helped me readjust to the American culture I had been totally out of contact with for over half a decade. (Remember, this was a time when even the Twin Towers were just in model form at the World's Fair.) Rob helped me to put together a slide presentation to use as I traveled around reconnecting with supporting churches. He taught me to use the latest technology to bring familiar African hyena sounds and lively African worship singing to American churches played through a modern cassette player along with reel-to-reel video footage. I had to synchronize the sound with the video by timing the start of the cassette player with the start of the reel-to-reel player, but I learned how. The people who watched and heard loved it.

Rob and I were offered the opportunity to go into real estate development and sales in Rochester, New York, during our time of reunion. The offer included building enough townhouses to sell several, while reserving three of them: one for my family, one for Rob's family, and a third one for the family of the man making the offer. Before committing to what seemed a perfect opportunity, I took time to seek the Lord for direction as I filled in for my in-laws' pastor during the month of January 1965. Not wanting to get caught in a trap to derail any assignment God had for us at specific times, I dug into the word and prayer to find out if it was time to go into real estate with my brother. As I sought the Lord, I read the story about Elisha and his servant Gehazi in II Kings 5. Part of what Elijah asked to Gehazi in that story, the Lord asked to me in my spirit as I read, "Is it a time to receive money . . . ?" (v5:26b, KJV). It was as though He breathed His voice right through those words. No, I knew this was not the right time to make or receive money. That time could wait. It was time to return to Kenya. I had received a clear direction through the written word. But before we returned we had the joy of helping to move Rob and Jan to New York City to assume leadership of the church our grandfather pioneered and pastored.

REFLECTION QUESTION:

When have you sacrificed something important to you for the sake of the Gospel?

CHAPTER 13

Back to Africa

Our second assignment to Kenya began in 1965 and lasted nearly five years. One day in October, our little family, along with Mary and Dave Clark and their family, boarded the *SS United States* and sailed four days to the port at Le Havre, France. From there we all took a train to Paris before parting ways. Our family went on to Rome, Italy, and Athens, Greece. Next, we flew to Addis Ababa, Ethiopia, when we decided to stay there a bit longer, stopping by to visit an older missionary friend. Our missionary friend Kenneth Oglesby knew Haile Selassie, Emperor of Ethiopia, quite well; therefore, the gracious emperor took us into his palace where he kept his pet lions. We took a picture of Mark and Marcia petting Selassie's chained lions. Finally, we flew on to our destination. We returned to Nairobi not because it was what was expected or because of what anyone else did, we returned because *we* knew we had not finished the work we went there to do.

In 1963 a revival had begun to spread among the students in Ethiopia. Pastor Winston Mattson Bose from Chicago visited Ethiopia on his way to Kenya in late 1965 hoping to find someone to speak into this new move of God. We recommended our Kenyan brother Chacha from the Wakuria people who worked with us and had taught himself Greek and Hebrew. He was a tremendous family man of God. He had moved from the bush area where he had grown up into the city of Nairobi where Gloria and I were living. We did not always agree (in fact, at times we even argued), but we trusted each other fully through mutual respect, genuine truthfulness, and active listening whether we agreed or not. I thought it better for Chacha to go into Ethiopia because we knew the Ethiopians did not have much trust for white people. What a successful match it proved. Chacha worked with some of the European missionaries on their compounds. One day as Chacha got up to preach at one particular mission compound, demon spirits began to cry out. Some female European missionaries tried their best to quiet the noisy spectators, but Chacha directed the ladies to leave the people alone. Having a black-skinned person telling white missionaries what to do did not go over well at the time, but Chacha continued on with his sermon proclaiming, "I am going to preach today about walking in the devil's territory!" As soon as he said that, more demons cried out. At the close of his preaching that day, Chacha cast those evil spirits out and many people were freed. A strong church was born out of the revival Chacha led, and Full Gospel Believers' Church lives today with many satellites. I traveled several times to Ethiopia to minister to the believers birthed out of Chacha's visit that sparked a strong national church. What a tremendous relationship he and I had to be able to impart life to each other along the way.

While we were away, All Nations Gospel Church had grown to some 300 people who had been forced out of the original renovated warehouse and into Rehemtula Hall, a 400-person capacity upstairs meeting room on bustling Jeevanjee Street. Because this church formed in bilingual roots during our first assignment, it continued with both English and Swahili services on the streets and in a common meeting place. Anyone and everyone who heard the message of the Gospel of Jesus Christ and responded was welcome. Upon our return this church body was growing in both numbers and depth of understanding. One day in 1965 as I walked the streets of Nairobi, I prayed for God to show me where to secure a building for all of the people inside the city being saved into His kingdom who couldn't possibly fit into the 400-person meeting hall. I told God I didn't have any money or political clout, but whatever He would tell me to do I would do. This impossible situation reminded me of the time Gramps had pointed out the plentiful breakfast provision right under my nose at Old Bridge. All I needed was for God himself to show me the provision this time. Directly, during a standing prayer at the corner of Government Road and Duke Street, the Lord's Spirit spoke clearly into my spirit, "I own the whole city." I knew right then God had a specific place and provision He would show me as I continued faithful to provide prophetic leadership to this church and move forward in faith. The words "I own the whole city" energized me so much that for the next few weeks I believed God would show me what to do next. Finally, I went looking for the land office building and located it. Not knowing one person inside, I walked right through the front door and down a hall where I spotted a door with a sign labeled "City Planning" when a youthful voice behind the closed door said, "Come in." The British were still serving in some key positions in the country in a very British way at this time. I proceeded to enter into the "City Planning" room and witnessed about twenty-five Kenyan men and women sitting behind drafting desks where they were drawing up plans for the city. I must have looked like a deer in headlights due to the shocking appropriateness of this place. As I scanned this room, to my left I noticed a door to another room with a sign attached marked "Mr. Farnsworth, Chief Evaluator." I took my good old time looking around the room and finally announced, "I have come here to see Mr. Farnsworth." I had no idea who Mr. Farnsworth was, but I knew which set-apart room he was in by the sign. I believed God was going before me, so I needed not to sit around doing nothing. One person who heard my announcement asked me if Mr. Farnsworth was expecting me. I told the inquirer, "No, but I have something really important to tell him." Mr. Farnsworth invited me right in to tell him the important news. I introduced myself and began talking to him about my really important topic. I told him that when the British came into Kenya the price of land rose out of reach to any African. I told him I knew of a group of Kenyans who were ready to build their own church, but would have no money left to build the church building after they had to pay for the expensive land on which they would build. He told me a law had been passed twenty years prior prohibiting granting land to a church or a mission. I told Mr. Farnsworth I appreciated his information, then I asked him to show me on a map the land I could not have, which was still available on that day and also would have been available twenty years prior if I had come in before the law had passed. Mr. Farnsworth led me back out into the drafting room where he pulled out a large, detailed map of Nairobi. He pointed out ten different pieces of land still owned by the Crown, and I wrote down specific addresses and lot numbers for ten "available" locations from the map. Next, I told the helpful gentleman from the evaluation office that I understood I was not allowed any of this land, but I was still going to go for the land anyway. Then I left.

After praying over my address list from Mr. Farnsworth's map and putting the sites in preference order from one to ten, I decided to write a letter to the city officials asking them to give our church the first location. They wrote me back stating that location had already been marked for an embassy. I wrote a second letter asking for the second location I had listed from the map. They notified me in another letter that a roundabout was slated to go onto that piece of property. I wrote a third letter requesting the third location from my list generated out of Mr. Farnsworth's office. They replied that land was owned by the railroad and that I need not continue writing them letters. I sent my next letter to the railroad asking for a specific piece of land right in the middle of the city. I waited a little while and when I did not hear back from the railroad, I myself went right to their main headquarters next to the train station in downtown Nairobi. When I knocked on the railroad headquarters' door, a British man with an arrogant attitude opened the door and snarled at me, "Who are you?" I replied, "I am from the church." I could tell my answer did not set well with him when he slammed the door in my face and yelled, "There is nothing for the church in here!"

I decided to go after the fourth location from my written list. That was the place God had in mind. Today All Nations Gospel Church stands on plot number four free of charge. Other church groups had tried to get land but were denied, even after appealing to the mayor or governor, but the miraculous happened when we moved by the Spirit of God. The results were impossible by human effort alone; we needed God to do the impossible and call things that were not as though they were because the results already were what He had in His mind.

Even after the Nairobi City Council gave us plot number four in the city center where hundreds of thousands of Kenyans walk by every day, I still had to walk wisely during the bureaucratic process for the land to transfer from them to us. Once the land became ours, we knew we would have to build immediately, so the elders of the Nairobi church asked for and worked toward another small, attached piece of land to slow down the process. We were ultimately denied the attached land, but the asking gave us two entire years to pray, prepare, and raise some money from the people who would be worshipping at All Nations for years to come.

We needed God to do the impossible!

As soon as the land was ours, we fenced it in and the women of the church and Gloria cleared the very rocky land. We hired an architect to draw up plans for the church similar to a church we looked at and liked in Mombasa. We sent these final plans out for an estimated cost for building the church. The estimate was so high it was in an alternate zone from our reality. We went back to the architect and told him we wanted to build the church ourselves with his blueprints, which we had paid him for. In that case, he refused to oversee the building project. I told him his decision was fine but that if we built it ourselves it would be better than the one he designed because we would not cut any corners on materials or best practices. I began to search for someone to build the building for us. Finally, I went to see an Indian builder friend of mine. He told me it would cost $125,000 if we hired him. It was still too much in my estimation, so I immediately prayed to the Lord for help.

My builder friend then said, as he pointed to a small man sitting barely noticeable in a dark corner of the room, "I can't do it for the price you have in mind, but that guy over there can do it." After the second Indian man stood, I was surprised to see he reached only about five feet, two inches tall even with the extra height of the turban wrapped around his head. This small man informed me he had already looked at our church building plans. I asked him what building experience he had, and he asked me if I was familiar with Nairobi's Barclay's bank! I sure was familiar with this great building he told me he had built. He went on to say he had left the country in 1963 because the prospects for Indians in Kenya weren't good at the time of its independence. However, when four years had passed, he saw Kenya once again as a land of opportunity and returned. He had a new Peugeot truck and a new cement mixer all ready and waiting for his first job back in Kenya and was ready to start his first job "for God." He then offered to provide the labor to build the church for just $10,000 if I would supply the materials! I hired him on the spot. Just then I heard a big crash outside the architect's office. A car had run over my trusty motor scooter and crushed it! After looking over the situation, I called over some young men standing nearby to help me lift the front of the crashed car off of my scooter. I crawled under the lifted car to pull out what was left of my two-wheeled transport. I stood dazed next to a woman carting chickens and waited for a local bus to take me home. So, you're going to build what? I heard the enemy whisper into my mind. At that, my faith and resolve settled. If the devil was going to this much trouble to try to stop me now, I knew I must not fail to obey God.

I purchased and supplied all the necessary materials for this precious Hindu man to construct All Nations Gospel Church in Nairobi, Kenya, for an approximate price of 45,000 US dollars. A wonderful Elim friend by the name of Joe Westbury from Atlanta, Georgia, donated $15,000 over time to help fund the project. The people from All Nations raised another $15,000 toward the cost. We collected the remaining $15,000 from various donors including a $1,000 gift from Lima Baptist Church in Lima, New York. Only God could have put that financial pack-

age together. Just as I was finishing up this church building project, Oral Roberts ministry people asked if I could help them set
up a crusade in Nairobi. I agreed with one stipulation—Oral
Roberts had to dedicate our new church. He agreed, so I secured
a stadium and coordinated bus transportation and everything
else his ministry needed for a large crusade. At this same time, I
ran the logistics for and taught at Nairobi Pentecostal Bible
School. After just nine months of construction, on one memorable Saturday, July 20, 1968, at 2:00 p.m., Dr. Oral Roberts dedicated All Nations Gospel Church right in the heart of Nairobi.
Fifteen-hundred people attended the dedication service inside
the building and another 1000 or so attended outside.

In order to prepare the church for dedication, Gloria and
other women in the church polished the cement floors using
dried half-shell coconuts and backbreaking effort. The major
changes, however, came years later when one woman's child was
healed from a chronic infirmity through prayer in that church.
Years later that same mother paid for the entire church floor to
be tiled. Another change came after one of the guards was mur-
dered on the church's front steps. In order to prevent that from
happening again, the striking, colorful bougainvillea surrounding
the original structure had to be changed into a 12-foot high wall
with jagged, broken glass cemented into its top for safety purposes. Today the church continues strong and unchanged from
its original purpose right in the middle of the bustling city center.
The building still holds 1500 people, has a surrounding balcony,
and an unshakeable concrete structure. In fact, the Nairobi Central District is the strongest Elim Fellowship body in Kenya because from the very beginning we encouraged it to stand on its
own two feet like any healthy, growing life does.

While Gloria and I focused on intentionally building unshakeable foundations in God's church, we became quite shook
up a couple of times when unexpected circumstances crept in
surrounding Marcia. One day our family visited the Nairobi National Park with another missionary family when, suddenly, an
adult baboon picked up our four-year-old Marcia, who was snack-

ing on a banana, and slowly started to carry her away out of the picnic area we were in. Before the baboon made it with Marcia to the nearest tree, we realized he was only after the banana. Gloria and I yelled with all our might, "Throw down the banana!" She did. The baboon dropped her and picked up the banana. Marcia ran as fast as she could back to us. It was a scary moment, but turned out fine because Marcia instantly listened and obeyed. In this case, obedience certainly proved better than sacrifice!

Periodically, we went on holiday to Mombasa where we rented a very crude house on the beach. The house was graced with two palm trees growing behind its mud walls and out its thatched roof. As I stated earlier, we made it a habit to go on these vacations at the same time as our good friends Dave and Mary Clark and their children so we could spend some quality time together remembering past times like when Mary borrowed Gloria's wedding dress for her wedding just one week after our wedding or our shared days spent in Bible school. We feel comforted by these great memories since both Dave and Mary have now gone to their home in heaven.

One of our Mombasa holidays proved to be more of a nightmare than a vacation. In August of 1966 we vacationed in Mombasa and were invited to stay in an apartment owned by Bud and Fay Sickler located on a single, narrow road leading to the airport. After a refreshing rest in Mombasa, Gloria and I began to pack up our belongings. Soon Mark and Marcia were invited to visit the three missionary children living across the street. We gave them permission to go, thinking this would give us time to finish packing the car to return to Nairobi. After saying goodbye to their friends, all five of the children ran to the edge of the road with Marcia lagging behind. The first four looked and crossed. When Marcia finally arrived at the edge of the road, she looked to her left. She saw nothing. She looked to her right. She saw a car and waited until it passed. She ran to cross, but was stopped by another fast-moving car coming from her left. The Japanese driver slammed on his brakes creating a screeching skid on the sizzling pavement, but his effort to stop the collision was too late. The car slammed into little Marcia, throwing her about 65 feet forward onto the pavement. Gloria and I watched helplessly as Marcia catapulted through the air before landing on the tarmac. The intensity of our screams reached heaven before we reached little, unconscious Marcia. The traumatized driver pounded on the street and wailed in grief. I simply placed my arms underneath her limp body and prayed, "Lord, we need a miracle, but we give you the choice. It is either a miracle of healing in her life or a miracle of grace in our life." As we stood there in shock, a woman offered to drive us to the nearest hospital. I quickly entered the back seat of her car with six-year-old Marcia in my arms. Gloria stayed behind with the missionary family staying across the street who later drove her to the same hospital. This particular hospital practiced English-style medicine which, at that time, thought best practice was to wait and see what happened before doing anything preemptive. Because Marcia was so restless, the hospital staff hesitated to find out the exact diagnosis right away. She remained unconscious for three very long days. The Japanese driver who hit Marcia came in to visit the children's ward to find out if she was still alive. We assured him she was indeed still alive. He left and returned in just a bit with the biggest doll he could find. We all waited for two weeks with no medicine or treatment from the hospital staff. Finally, at the end of just two weeks, Marcia walked out of the hospital. It was a true miracle! Her doctor was now ready to make a diagnosis. He inquired, "Tell me how she was hit." I told him that the car smashed into her. He replied he thought she had just fallen into the car. Marcia was finally diagnosed with a compression break of her left wrist. This accident was a major event in our lives that we were only able to get through by the grace flowing from His right arm and holy hand upholding us in the same fashion I had held little, helpless Marcia.

Also in 1966, we lived in a nice, little house in Nairobi. At the same time, Eva Butler, daughter of Ivan Q. Spencer, had been living in Kenya with her two children since about 1950. She had started girls' schools in South Nyanza, in Bukuria and Suna Mission stations, not too far from where we were now living. Now, Eva sensed a burden to take the full Gospel to the Maasai about 70 miles to the south of us. She proceeded to ask me and PEFA overseer Chacha Omahe about going to the Maasai. Chacha and Eva took a few trips out to Maasai country until they found a good place for her to live where the government had drilled a bore hole at a place named Mashuru. Eva agreed that was a good spot because the Maasai would come there for water. I played a role situating Eva south of us into her new assignment among the Maasai. Through my contacts in the government and church, I was able to secure an old 13 by 15 foot corrugated metal house free of charge. I assembled the hut right on a hill near the bore hole, creating a center for Eva. She moved in for the next three or four years before building a more permanent house. She later wrote a book about her experience entitled *In the Shadow of Kilimanjaro: Pioneering the Pentecostal Testimony among the Maasai People* where on pages 41 and 42 she recalls her move from her vantage point:

> After three months, in August 1966, Paul finally got the shanty of corrugated iron sheets 13 1/2' by 15 1/2', the roof in two parts, one gable and down on either side, the walls in sections. They loaded it on a lorry and we packed up two cars. We needed our beds, a table and chairs, and household goods to start house-keeping. Chacha, Paul, his co-pastor Brother Samuel Mwatha, and we two ladies set out. It was something. We knew one road, which wasn't the best. We found another one, and better ones later. We took the second road and finally arrived, letting the headmaster know we had come. We pulled up between the rocks and unloaded. They had brought two-foot square cement slabs, about two inches thick, for a floor. They started in, leveled the ground, put sand down and started to erect the building. That was about midday. We ladies fixed something to eat. We had supper and the head-master let us camp out in the schoolrooms that night

as it was a term break. Next day the men worked all morning finishing the building, and laid the flooring blocks, putting some outside the door for a frontage. Our house was erected. After lunch and prayer for us, they left and we began to scrub the walls of that shanty and worked at it until late afternoon . . . .

In the morning, the cook was on hand. He came to the door and knocked. When I opened he said, 'Madam, you had visitors last night.'

'Who?' I asked.

'Come see.'

The car was parked just down a few steps. All around the car were large pad tracks, where a lion had inspected it. Then up closer to our door was a bag of charcoal; he had come up to smell that out as well.

Well, what you don't see and what you don't hear doesn't hurt you.

Over the next few years I had a number of opportunities to dedicate new church buildings. At times our family had to walk through herds of impalas and zebras to get to these Maasai churches, but it was well worth the time and effort.

———•••———

Eva was living in her hut when she met three Maasai boys all wearing only what looked like big bath towels hanging around their necks. Paul and I later learned these were not bath towels at all, but rather clothing called *shukas*. These three boys had had some schooling, so Eva invited them to go to a Bible school called Independent Pentecostal Assemblies about 200 miles west of us. It was the school in Kaimosi where Dave and Mary Clark served. One evening Eva stopped by our house on her drive to Kaimosi with the three boys, David, Paul, and William, dressed in their *shukas* and red dirt infused hair. I did not know they were coming, so I offered them what I had prepared for our supper—

spaghetti—of which I had plenty. These young Maasai boys had been used to a very different diet consisting mostly of corn, meat, and milk with blood. The eight of us ate around our table that night. Months later one of the boys said to me, "You know, Mama, when we ate at your house we thought you were serving us worms!" It was a riot! I had no idea they never before had seen meatballs, sauce, bread, and "white worms." I thought of all the amazing eating out we had done in Kenya when we ate foods for the very first time like stuffed goat intestines. Thankfully, that meal was finished off with familiar lemon meringue pie. Other first foods for me were the common, rubbery cow's udder and my personal least favorite sweet tea boiled with milk and sugar over an open fire. The first time I tasted its strong, smoky flavor was in Bukuria at the mission station. That was just the first of many times I tasted that particular tea recipe since it was a common drink in that rural area. At first, if I was able to drink the tea, it was only after allowing it to cool completely. Sometimes I skipped ingesting it by allowing the dirt floor to secretly soak up the mixture after I discreetly poured it out onto the dirt or I gave it to Paul to drink as I continued on eating my *ugali* (ground corn meal cooked firm and hand eaten). The only tea I had before in Michigan was regular hot green tea made by my mother. As difficult as it was, by the time I left Bukuria I could drink as many cups of that sweet tea as anyone else. God graced me with a special change of palate as I kept on drinking the smoky sweet tea. Other food-related difficulties I overcame were the difficult smells and the corroded tin cups that looked to me more like a chemistry experiment than a shared teacup. The locals used river water in cooking, but our water came from the rain water collected in two big, cement vats located on the eaves of our house's roof. I still had to boil and filter the water before I could use it in cooking. The effort was worth it, though, because out in the bush even the milk had to be boiled and strained. Just basic living in the bush was a lot of work. In addition to boiling water and milk, I kept potassium permagnum tablets to wash all raw foods in to make them safe for eating.

When we first arrived in Bukuria, Mark was still drinking formula out of a bottle, which saved me some work. As soon as he was weaned from the bottle, everything any of us ate or drank was the result of tons of work. In Nairobi, the cultural food shock was not as intense because the Kikuyu tribe fixed a lot of stews. I had grown up on not so different stews in the cold Michigan climate of my hometown.

———•••———

As Gloria and I went along life's way, we learned "Never allow your lifestyle to hijack your calling." This is a principle we have applied to our lives meaning calling comes before lifestyle always.

My sister Marilyn moved to Nairobi and into our home from 1967 through 1969. Marilyn had her master's degree in education and was employed by the school system on Long Island when the Nairobi school system invited her to a teaching position. The school system on Long Island released her, giving her a two-year contract to work in Nairobi and agreeing to reinstate her upon her return as though there were no break at all.

> *"Never allow your lifestyle to hijack your calling."*

As long as she was right there with us, it was my desire to expand the Sunday school into new areas; therefore, I asked her to train some teachers at church. I noticed an Elim church in Mombasa had an active Sunday school program. That church hired buses to drive into the city to pick up children to bring back to church and then return to their homes. The teachers gave these five-hundred or so children candy. When the leaders of this program asked me how many children we had in our Sunday school program, I told them a hundred and twenty-five. Rather than giving the children candy, I thought, why not do something to make them actually want to come to Sunday school? That was where my sister came in to help. Marilyn led an intense Sunday school teacher training program for several months. At the completion of the teachers' training, we held a graduation ceremony to honor thirty-four new teachers. Ahead of the graduation I bought a big sheet of 4 x 8 Masonite reminiscent of the Masonite my dad once used to create our family's temporary camper trailer. This time I painted the whole sheet of Masonite with blackboard paint and cut it up into equal 18 by 24 inch rectangles. Now they had portable blackboards. My next step was to hire a man to sew carrying bags for the miniature blackboards. He sewed up a stylish bag big enough to hold chalk, an eraser, a flannel board, and a portable blackboard. I had certificates of graduation printed up. Each and every teacher received not only a professional looking certificate he or she could be proud of, but also a school-in-a-bag at the graduation ceremony in front of the whole church on one Sunday morning. My message that day to those teachers was the following: "Wherever you see kids, teach." We dedicated them to teach. It wasn't a matter of bringing the children into the church, it was a matter of taking the church out to where they were and giving them something lasting. We must not sacrifice the future, simply to enjoy the present. Out of the hundred plus churches today in Nairobi born out of the original All Nations Gospel, many of those churches started from these thirty-four well-trained visionary teachers. Our Sunday school-in-a-bag spread out into the masses throughout the four corners of Nairobi. We must always see the big picture.

On the 300 mile drive from Nairobi to Mombasa a traveler may be able to see elephants on the road, as well as to catch a glimpse of the snow covered top of Mount Kilimanjaro off to the right side of the road on the Kenya and Tanzania border. Every time I drove by that dormant volcano on my many travels, I would think about how much I wanted to climb it to the very top. Finally, in 1967, about three years before we moved back to the United States, I and a few of my friends together climbed Mount Kilimanjaro from the less traveled Kenya side. My sister

Marilyn joined our hiking group on this occasion. We set out from Nairobi and traveled by car the approximate 125 miles to the foot of the highest cone on the Kenya side. On foot we hiked up in about three-and-a-half days. When we reached the mountain's top at over 19,200 feet above sea level, we sat down to catch our breath because the oxygen was very thin. We had not taken any portable oxygen with us because we were already somewhat acclimated to a higher altitude from our time spent living in Nairobi at 6000 feet above sea level. It only took us a day and a half to descend. We slept in open-mouthed caves during the entire five day trip up and down.

The work in Nairobi was very draining: starting a Bible school, setting up a huge crusade, receiving new missionaries, and saying farewell to others going on leave. Constructing the church building in Nairobi took nine months of intense work to finish in order to prepare for the Oral Roberts crusade. I found myself drained of spiritual and emotional energy. The whole time we were there, there were no Christian conferences, workshops, et cetera, for us to attend for encouragement and refilling. I had to draw upon the Lord alone. It was five-and-a-half years before I was able to sit under, listen to, and receive a Christian message. Thankfully, Gloria and I were able to dig spiritual wells deep enough to handle years of drought. (We are still drawing on those wells.) God dug one of those deep spiritual wells through my soul in a very surprising way. It was during this long season of drought that I thought I really needed to spend time in prayer with spiritual brothers. My mind immediately went to other white missionaries, and I pictured only white missionaries praying for me. It is amazing how and when God shows us the bias that is in our hearts. The Holy Spirit convicted me of this bias revealed against the very people I loved. I repented and called the elders of the Nairobi church

> *We must always see the big picture.*

together. I asked them to lay hands on me and pray for refreshment for my emotions and spirit. They were more than willing to help. We spent three hours ministering one to another. It was like splashing in a desert oasis. Thankfully, I dug a deep spiritual well with my Kenyan brothers and called together the elders every three months thereafter for mutual prayer and encouragement before carrying on.

One man added to God's kingdom during the street evangelization during our first stay in Nairobi was a one-eyed Kikuyu Mau Mau fighter. He knelt down on a Nairobi street one day and gave his life to Jesus Christ. When I finally met him at All Nations Gospel during this, our second assignment in Nairobi, I asked this brother how he ended up with a glass eye. He told me his story about being a Mau Mau hiding out like an animal in the forest. The British painted themselves black so they could enter the forest undetected where he lived. Anything these British soldiers saw move, they shot. One day a bullet flew right through his blind of leaves into his eye and out through his cheek. To avoid the dogs and police, he immediately ran to a little stream to bathe his eye. He packed his injury with mud and his heart with fierce anger toward his white attackers. He finally left the forest for the city where he heard some of our "crazy" people preaching. He left those "crazy" preaching people when he came upon some more of our "crazies." Finally, he said he came to a group of people where I was preaching about the love of Jesus Christ when, at our church's preaching site closest to our church, something miraculous happened to him. He finally saw past his blind hate for whites and his misinterpretations of "crazy" people to hear some really good news: Jesus died and rose again so he could live in peace and safety in eternity. What a wonderfully anger-free, serious-minded Christian he became. Because we had returned to Kenya, I was able to meet this living fruit from our past labor.

Seeing the big picture, Gloria and I transferred Mark and Marcia from St. George's Primary School, a British school, into Rosalyn Academy, an American Mennonite day school on the edge of Nairobi, for the 1968 to 1969 school year. Marcia was going into grade 3 and Mark was going into grade 6. Mark excelled in various sports during his school days, especially soccer, cricket, track, high-jump, rugby, and field hockey at both St. George's and Rosalyn. Marcia, the socialite, was always involved in all kinds of group activities. The Rosalyn school used American curriculum, which helped to transition Mark and Marcia from the English system to the American system. We wanted them to be prepared for when we moved back to the United States and attending Rosalyn did just that for them.

Before Nairobi Pentecostal Evangelistic Fellowship of Africa Bible School formed, Elim-related Bible schools in Kenya only ran for three-month training sessions. I knew it took more than three months to establish a solid biblical foundation for ministry. If God truly had "many people in this city" as I believed He did, then His people needed access to long-term, solid Bible training if they were going to grow to full maturity. It just so happened at the time I was pondering this need that Cyril Cross and his wife Barbara from the British Assemblies of God arrived in Nairobi. They had been serving in the Congo, but as a result of the uprising there, they unexpectedly moved to Kenya and settled in with the Elim people in Nairobi. Cyril and I joined with our brothers Chacha Omahe and Pastor Samuel Mwatha to prayerfully meet the need to establish a three-year-long Bible training school. And that is how the long-term, three-year solid Nairobi PEFA Bible School began. As PEFA developed into a well-recognized and established organization, leaders chose Chacha Omahe to be the Nairobi overseer. He was well prepared to handle those coming to join only for the money. For example, a group of twelve pastors once came to him asking for PEFA membership. He was able to communicate to them that after ten years of being independent, how could they just now be deciding to join PEFA? "You can't join us," he told them. "You go back and think about your decision and then call us within the next two months and we'll talk some more." They never called!

Although this process took longer, it ended up saving many avoidable problems and producing a stronger, long-term unity in PEFA. Looking back I can see that this one adjustment Gloria and I committed to in Nairobi—not allowing anyone to depend on people as their source of provision—was a key to long-term success.

As a part of getting to know each other, Cyril Cross and I began to discuss the glaring need for Bible literacy to accompany the move of the Holy Spirit happening in Kenya. Many people who knew very little to nothing of God's word were being saved by the Spirit. Cyril and I saw eye-to-eye. Kenya needed a much longer Bible school program. We agreed Cyril's gifting and experience made him the perfect fit to be in charge of the programming, while my gifting and experience made me the perfect fit to coordinate all of the logistics. As Gramps had taught me so many years before, when there is a job to be done no one needs to be standing around idle. Immediately in 1966, I decided to drive around the city to see what I could find for a building as my first step forward. Finally, I spotted a large, lonely stone house with three rooms. I inquired as to the owner who, I was told, was a Jewish man by the name of Bwana Hirschfield who owned 5000 farm acres where he grew coffee surrounding the stone house. I did a bit more investigating to find out where Bwana Hirschfield lived. Once I found that out, I drove to his plantation home and introduced myself. He invited me in for tea and, of course, I accepted the offer because tea time is a great, relaxing time to talk, and talk we did. I told him about my plan to start a Bible school in Nairobi where people could study the Bible for a few years, especially the Old Testament and after that the New Testament. He appeared to be especially agreeable to the Old Testament study. I asked him what his plans were for his old stone coffee house. He said he had no plans, so I replied that I could use it. He granted me free use, which perfectly matched our budget even though we had to install electricity and run water from about 300 feet away. It really was not large enough for what I envisioned, but it was a great start: two medium-sized classrooms, a dining room in the middle, and a very small kitchen. I started the renovations by solving the easiest problem first; I made sure the building had electricity. Next, I bought 300 feet of water piping to run in an 18-inch underground trench connected to the city water. There was an exposed brass water meter one of the men had to sleep on all night to protect. We were making major progress in a short time. Again I could see that it was God's right hand and His holy arm working right along with us.

I finally tracked down Elias Irungo, a second-in-command cook, who had been working at a nearby hospital. He was now in jail. I went down to the jail to visit him. The doors clanged before the slim, bald-headed man came to me. His countenance was downcast. I asked him for his story. He told me how the chief cook was Luo and he was Kikuyu. He explained how he rebuked the devil in his chief cook and was subsequently reprimanded. Finally, one day while he was cutting some meat, this chief cook walked in and Elias shook a knife in his face. The police were called immediately, and that is how he ended up in jail.

After I listened to his story I asked, "Can you obey what I tell you?" He replied, "Yes."

I said, "I will help you," and presently informed the jail keeper, "I am taking this man with me." I proceeded to escort Elias right out of that lockup and into a job. And that is how Elias Irungo found his assignment as our trusted cook.

Elias saw evil spirits in students when he came to work at the school, and he would tell the students so without any concern for tact. I quickly told our new devil-hunting cook, "You are called to this room (pointing to the kitchen). Outside this room, you will not prophesy or tell people they have demons." He obeyed, so I learned to trust him to do the exact job I instructed, which was cooking. I had complete confidence in his cooking. As a result, Elias was able to cook unrestrained. I loved this man past his flaw.

I still needed a place for the students to stay. I decided to travel a mile away to Kariobungi and to rent a residential house to serve as the dormitory. I got right at filling the house with single beds, basic amenities, and the first sixteen students. Our campus was now one mile across from the rented house "dormitory" to the rent-free coffee house "campus center." Thus, a three-year Kenyan Bible school was born. If Cyril Cross had not been rescued by mercenaries out of the eastern Congo and transported by lorry to Nairobi at just the right time and if I had not returned to Nairobi for a second time at just the same right time, then Nairobi Pentecostal Evangelistic Fellowship of Africa Bible School may not exist today. It does, though, because Cyril, our African brothers, and I walked together in the footsteps of Abraham's faith.

Our enrollment the first year was about sixteen students, and that number almost doubled by the second year of 1969. For the first year and a half of the Bible school's existence, I oversaw its operations, while Cyril served as principal and curriculum developer. Our trusted African brothers taught and counseled the students, along with Gloria and Marilyn teaching weekly. Out of this little campus startup came great preachers who not only evangelized in Kenya, but also throughout Europe and South Africa. One of our notable graduates was Arthur Kitonga, who went on to start thousands of churches all over the world. Arthur is just one of the many powerhouses fully trained at Nairobi PEFA Bible School.

It was midsummer 1969 and time for my family and me to return to the United States so I could further my education. My job as Bible school coordinator complete, my job instilling principles like "Don't ever be bought by anyone!" into the curriculum complete, my job setting up a Sunday school teacher training complete, but what was not complete, nor ever will be complete, is my continual love and concern for the Kenyan people, which is why I felt such a concern for the young, three-year Bible school as we went to leave. However, thanks be to God, Cyril and Barbara Cross from the British Assemblies of God shared our burden, investing time, money, and personnel to carry the school forward. In fact, they purchased a 5-acre piece of land with a house already on it and added a beautiful two-story dormitory with classrooms, a chapel, and a teachers' residence included, eventually renaming the growing school the

Nairobi Pentecostal Bible College. I will always be grateful God provided the right people at the right time to carry the Bible school vision forward when Gloria, the children, and I moved back to our country of origin in 1969.

Gloria and I were at peace with the work we had left behind to others in Kenya. George and June Lindsay, along with many qualified African brethren, oversaw the work in Central Province. Senior missionary Bud Sickler oversaw the spread of the Gospel throughout Kenya and Tanzania, and Pastor Samuel Mwatha oversaw the young Nairobi church dependent on its own indigenous principles for raising funds. Again, after the three years we spent working for the TL Osborn organization and watching the dependency created by systematic financial support from outsiders, Gloria and I decided right from the start we would model a different pattern in any work we founded. We did not want anyone to become dependent on us. We did see that start-up money was needed when there was no seed money at all, so we did help out from time to time, but beyond that we did not want to create a co-dependent weakness in the work. This saved us many problems. At the same time it increased our faith as we then had to believe God for dedicated local workers who would give all of themselves and all of their resources for the sake of the ministry.

One last special event took place before we returned to the United States in 1969. The people whom we came to know and to love threw a tea party for us. The menu for a Kenyan tea party consisted of jam sandwiches, cookies, and tea. It was quite an honor. They left us with these parting words: "Brother Johansson is our teacher. He is our father. But our mother is Gloria Johansson. She has taught us so much, and she knows what is under our beds." We had become their mother and father in the Lord. Culturally it is improper to go into the bedroom of someone else's home, but because they accepted Gloria as part of their family, they acknowledged that she even knew what was under their beds! What an honor to be so accepted. We may have been raised in a different culture, but our cultures did not get in the way of our becoming one family in the kingdom of God with our family in Kenya. The differences that had seemed so stark upon our arrival had faded into our mutual love and respect. Truly by giving up precious time with our natural families in the United States our family grew so that now we were not only a part of the Johansson family and the Smith family, we now had all of the many families in Kenya as a precious part of our extended, Christian family. We knew we had many homes to stay in whenever we were to return, and we knew our Kenyan family would be staying with us whenever they visited our homeland. Oh, how our family had grown.

There were hundreds of Kenyan Christians who saw us off at the airport. These precious brothers and sisters gathered from various organizations in order to bid us farewell. One of the leaders (from an organization besides Elim) told me I was a part of them, so I must return. Witnessing this crowd and hearing their words of support, made me know in my heart that they had affected a change in Gloria and me to live our lives with a focus on people and not programs.

Now it was our time to return to the United States in 1969 and we were able to stop by England for a few days before returning home.

REFLECTION QUESTION:

Can you recall a time when you sacrificed the present in exchange for a better future?

Wedding in Jackson, Michigan, November 10, 1956

Meshoppen, PA: First pastorate, 1956

Carlton & Elizabeth Spencer Farewell: March, 1959

Crossing the Atlantic

Our first VW— Burkuria, 1959

Home at Burkuria Mission, 1959

at Burkuria Mission

Gloria with Maasai woman

Hospital in Kisumu, Kenya

Marcia, born in Kisumu, Kenya

13' python

4½' cobra

Paul crossing the river

Building, bush-style

Burkuri Missions Boy's Education with Gloria

BUKURIA MISSION
ELIM
MISSIONARY ASSEMBLIES

Paul with Mark and Marcia at Balmoral House

Egypt

Marcia and Mark in Israel

Berlin Wall

Return to Kenya, 1965

Farewell to our families, 1965

SS United States

Celebrating Mark's 8th birthday on the SS United States

Back in Nairobi

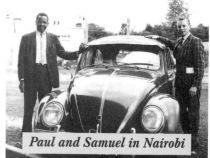

Paul and Samuel in Nairobi

Pioneering a church downtown

Nairobi church elders

Nairobi residence

Second meeting hall in Nairobi

Training Seminars

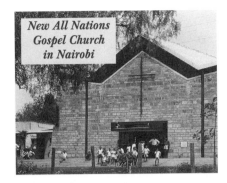

New All Nations Gospel Church in Nairobi

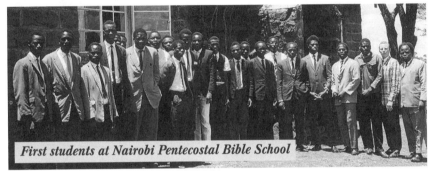

First students at Nairobi Pentecostal Bible School

Balmoral House in Nairobi

Mark with All Nations church van

Teacher Training Class

Climbing Mt. Kilimanjaro

Eva Butler

Paul visiting Maasai boma (hut)

Pastor Samuel & Mary with us

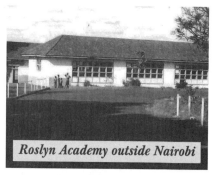

Roslyn Academy outside Nairobi

Gloria at street meeting

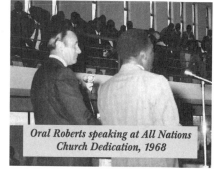

Oral Roberts speaking at All Nations Church Dedication, 1968

SECTION IV
EXTENDING OUR HORIZON

CHAPTER 14

Roundabout to Elim

It was July 1969. Neil Armstrong landed on the moon, and Gloria, 12-year-old Mark, 9-year-old Marcia, and I landed back at Elim Bible Institute. The temperature ranged about ten degrees above normal as we settled back into New York, making our transition a wee bit softer. Before returning to the United States, I had agreed to take the responsibility of dean of men at my alma mater Elim Bible Institute. I previously decided to pursue a bachelor's degree when I returned, so I immediately enrolled in Roberts Wesleyan College in Chili, New York. My schedule was full to overflowing when I heard that the indigenous financial pattern I had implemented back at All Nations Gospel in Nairobi hit a glitch when the senior missionary in charge decided to return to the old pattern of financial support from the United States. The problem was all of the pastors Gloria and I had trained refused to go back to the old pattern, which then created great tension. One of the local leaders informed me by telegram of the conflict, which led to my calling an elders' meeting on the Elim campus because of the depth of disappointment I felt. I initially thought it was a perfect meeting time because the senior missionary on the one side of the tension happened to be in the United States where he could listen as I explained my point of view in front of him and the Elim elders. It turned out not to be the perfect meeting in that this senior missionary did not seem to change his mind at all, explaining he was fearful the new church building might fall into the wrong hands and he wanted to keep it as a missionary holding. We had reached an impasse when, that night in prayer alone, I sensed the Spirit prompt me to say that I took full responsibility for any misunderstanding and conflict. The meeting ended with the elder Elim brethren rejoicing over a resolution. I had been in prayer and knew that in the long-run God would vindicate the financial principles Gloria and I had firmly established before we left. The Elim elders suggested I write a letter to the African pastors encouraging them to be at peace and to continue in fellowship with the senior missionary while continuing to make provision for the new indigenous way they had been taught by Gloria and me. I sent that letter and followed it with a trip to ensure the principles were being peacefully followed. I knew that if I obeyed God, doing what He told me to do by the principles of his Word, the leaders would be empowered. Not only was I convinced they would be empowered spiritually by the Holy Spirit, but they would also be lifted up in their faith, thereby allowing them to stand on their own two, mature feet. In the end, I knew they would succeed despite conflict and struggle. And that is exactly what happened over the long haul. These pastors and their flocks are much stronger today for having established themselves on a solid indigenous foundation and not on shaky foreign support. Also at that time, I felt my obedience to resolve the conflict would open the doors not only in Kenya, but also throughout Africa. God responded to my obedience by opening doors immediately that eventually led to invitations into African nations from the top of the continent all the way through to the bottom.

It took me about two-and-a-half years to earn my bachelor's degree in history, all the while helping to care for our two children, ministering weekends at various churches and conferences, counseling, and as dean of men overseeing the growing number of students at Elim. As I approached my graduation from Roberts Wesleyan in 1972, I took time to prayerfully seek God's will for my future. Should I proceed immediately with another degree? Or, should I take my family and return to Kenya? I needed an answer from above. One consideration was our teenage children who needed to feel settled for their emotional stability.

It became clear God desired for me to pursue another degree right away. Since I had been so involved in Kenya, I decided the most beneficial degree would be a master's in African history in order that when I returned to Kenya I would be able to benefit the Kenyan people with a wider perspective concerning their own background. While living in Kenya, I had noticed that many Kenyans viewed their historical beginning with the coming of the white man. In reality, I knew the entire African continent had an ancient history with many authentic accounts written by Arab historians. But before I started another round of school, in the summer of 1972 I was invited by Ralph Mahoney to speak at World Map's California camp meetings, so I decided to take our family on a cross-country trip to California, visiting most of the national parks along the way including Yellowstone National Park and the Grand Canyon.

I futilely began to search for a school somewhere in the Rochester area that offered courses in African studies. Finally, I drove to Brockport State University just west of Rochester, New York, and asked for the Lord's leading. I walked around the campus until I came upon the history department's office and to a door marked African Studies. I walked in, found a professor who happened to be a good Presbyterian, and began to tell him my life story set in Africa. After some delightful discussion, I went to leave when he stated, "If there is anything I can do for you, just let me know." Immediately, I proceeded to find the head of the history department. I informed him I wanted to earn a master's degree in African studies. He replied that though they were going to offer that program next year, there were many people waiting ahead of me, and the school was only accepting twenty students into the new program. I asked him how I could become one of those twenty before recalling what the Presbyterian professor had just told me. Then I asked him, "Would it help if a professor from this university invited me into the African studies program?" He replied, "Yes, definitely." I exited his office and reentered the first office where the friendly professor worked. After explaining what had happened in between my leaving his office the first time and coming back a second time, he gladly wrote an official letter inviting me into the school's African studies program. That was my key in, and I was able to take the majority of required courses needed taught by African professors. I put in my written requests for courses in African studies, East Africa and West Africa studies, South African, and ancient African studies, with a minor in 20th century America. Basically, I was able to design my own complete course of study. In just two hard-working years, I became the first student to graduate from Brockport with a master's degree in African history. In fact, I believe I was the first Brockport student to graduate with a master's in history!

Once again I found myself at a crossroads. Was it time to move on? Or, was it time to stay longer? I prayed and sought godly counsel from the Elim leadership. The Elim Fellowship elders deemed it wise for me to spend more time at Elim training missionary personnel and continuing to serve in a broader role as dean of students. Our children were settled into the local school and were looking forward to continuing on in that geographical area. This plan aligned with everything I knew to be true, right, and good, besides I felt as though we had just lived through three lifetimes in one relatively short period of time. I knew God was upholding me by His mighty right hand and holy arm through all the many assignments He had given me, but I had to take responsibility for my part, too, which was to stay laser-focused on the assignments at hand and to eliminate any and all frivolous distractions. It was during this laser-focused time that God added into my view Australia. I was invited by Revival Crusade, a major Australian Pentecostal denomination of the time, to minister as one of their keynote speakers. Accepting this invitation proved a positive, long-term connection. They even invited me back ten years later as their keynote speaker for their 50th anniversary celebration.

Our children enjoyed attending and graduating from Honeoye Falls/Lima High School in Honeoye Falls, New York, eventually both also graduating from Monroe Community College in Rochester with associate's degrees. As always, Gloria grew into a greater position of strength and leadership during this assignment. Wherever she lived she was a model of a wife who respected her husband and loved her children. She never was afraid to embrace the responsibilities of leading in church, school, or any other organization. She became a true leader of women at Elim.

In 1980 we built a house in Lima, New York, where we enjoyed living for four delightful years before moving to New York City. By this time our children were beginning to spread their wings. Mark met Mary. Mary was the wonderful daughter of Elim's Academic Dean Bob Mahaffey and his wife Maxine. Mark married Mary in 1977 after graduating from SUNY Geneseo in Livingston County, New York, and later earned a master's degree in education, which enabled him to land a teaching job in 1982 at Hampton Christian Academy in Hampton, Virginia. After years of teaching, he accepted the invitation to become a youth pastor with New Covenant Church, eventually assuming the position of senior pastor of this loving congregation for seventeen years until 2016 when he stepped away. For over ten years Gloria and I have had the privilege of belonging to this same wonderful church body pastored for years by our son. Mark truly is a pastor's pastor.

Mark and Mary had Andrew, born in Rochester, New York, and Katie, born in Newport News, Virginia. Once full grown and after becoming a physician's assistant, Andrew married Emily Black who blessed us with three great-grandchildren: Caleb, Hazel, and Levi. Andrew and Emily serve their local church in various capacities. We are so proud of them all.

Our only granddaughter Katie met Peter Stern, son of missionaries to Kenya, while they attended Elim Bible Institute. Upon graduation they married and now have children Eleanor and Lillian. Peter graduated from Regent University with a master's degree in digital media, and Katie earned a bachelor's degree from Roberts Wesleyan College in Rochester, New York. Peter now works as a computer designer at Newport News Shipyard in Virginia, while he and his wife also serve their local church in various ways. It has been wonderful having these grands and greats living nearby.

Our daughter Marcia graduated from Monroe Community College before marrying Bill Herlan, whom she had met on the

Elim campus. They were blessed with twin boys Paul and Ryan during their ten year marriage. Marcia eventually went on to graduate from the University of Rochester receiving a master's degree as a nurse practitioner in critical care and finally a Doctorate of Nursing Practices from the University of South Florida. During her time of practicing at Strong Memorial through the University of Rochester, Marcia trained alongside an Ethiopian intern.

Once that intern questioned Marcia, "Is my patient in yet?"

Marcia returned, "I am not your nurse. Get your own nurse."

He pushed, "Don't you know who I am?"

She responded, "Do you know who I am? In Ethiopia I petted Haile Selassie's lions."

After that she never had a problem with this intern. Her earlier experiences at the Ethiopian palace paid off at a hospital in Rochester, New York!

Marcia was able to finish her degrees, raise her boys, and enjoy life in part because we opened our home back up to her while we lived in Lima, New York. The desire to become a nurse began in Marcia when she was only four years old. My parents sent her a nurse's outfit for a gift. After wearing it, she said, "When I grow up, I am going to be a nurse." And so it came to pass.

Within five years of moving out on her own, Marcia came to a place where she was well set to support not only herself, but also her growing boys. Once her boys were fully grown and in college, in 2006 Marcia married John Marquardt, an orthopedic surgeon she met while working at Highland Hospital in Rochester, New York. The whole family attended their beautiful wedding held on the beach at Clearwater Beach, Florida. Not only did John and Marcia share a special commitment to serving God through health care, but they also shared the experiences that come along with parenting children of similar ages. This made it easier for their combined total of two grown daughters and three adult sons to integrate into their new family unit.

Later, Paul and Ryan both graduated from Houghton College in Houghton, New York. Paul continued to pursue medical training, eventually finishing as a physician's assistant and landing a full-time job in the cardiac unit of Johns Hopkins All Children's Hospital in St. Petersburg, Florida. Before landing his job, Paul married Keri Annable, who already had a master's degree in special education. Today they are the proud parents of sweet Guilliana.

Ryan went on from Houghton to RIT as part of Houghton's 4 + 1 program to finish his master's degree in business administration. Ryan married Jennifer Radon, who had a bachelor of arts degree in marketing. They now reside in St. Petersburg, Florida, where he works as an underwriter. Renley is their beautiful daughter.

Love God; help people.

Words, whether spoken or written, cannot fully express the pride and admiration Gloria and I feel toward our daughter Marcia who rose to the top above all of the unexpected adversity and pain hurled at her. She more than survived; she thrived.

We are very proud of both of our children, all four of our grandchildren, and, as of right now, our eight great-grandchildren aged six years and under. To all of them and any additional offspring to come, we leave four very important words: "Love God; help people."

REFLECTION QUESTION:

What few words would you leave for a future generation?

CHAPTER 15

New York School of Urban Ministry (NYSUM)

It was the Thanksgiving season of 1976 when I first decided to drive the family from Lima, New York, to New York City. Gloria and I were busy serving at Elim where an Ethiopian student named Philipos was studying. It just so happened Philipos needed a ride to the City to visit his friends, so we offered to let him ride along with us. The drive to New York City proved pretty unremarkable, but what happened after I dropped Philipos off and walked around the back of our car was quite remarkable. Once we reached his building in Manhattan, I thought it polite to walk Philipos to the door. What I discovered behind the door when it opened was a treasure full of Ethiopian culture I had never before witnessed in the City. I exited the building with an encouraging surprise in my heart and, as I walked around the rear of my car to get on with the trip, I was taken further by surprise when I sensed the Spirit of God speak clearly into my spirit, "You will open a school for culture and urban ministry."

What I did not know was when I would open such a school. Like most people who hear a true *rhema* (divine word), I thought it would happen quickly and the fulfillment of the vision God gave me appeared to be in sight. After three years of waiting, my brother Rob, who was pastoring in New York City and who shared the vision, found a building on 46th and Broadway in Queens that seemed to be ideal for such a use. The building was up for auction so Rob went to check the building out and we both began to pray. Much to our dismay, the building went to another buyer. Against all hope, Rob and I both still believed this was indeed the building we would own to begin an urban school for culture and ministry. We continued to wait and pray for seven more long years until that building would become available again.

In 1983 I was flying weekly from Rochester to New York City when I was invited by Pastor Jim Cymbala to start a Bible school at Brooklyn Tabernacle. There I had the privilege of teaching *Romans, Hebrews, Acts,* and other biblical topics to thousands of New Yorkers. After years of praying and fasting at lunch time every Tuesday with different Elim campus students and staff like Dr. John Smucker, I was impressed in my spirit that this was the year Gloria and I would be making the move to begin a new urban school. I knew God had heard the fervent prayers of people like Judy Ebersole and Rosemary Esch. Soon, my brother called me from the City to inform me the building we desired was up for sale again. We knew the time was *now.* Ten years since the initial seed was planted, the door to the building that closed seven years prior opened wide again; however, in the meantime, the building had been vandalized and had fallen into desperate need of repair. Perhaps this was the very reason we were now able to purchase this building for just $165,000. We were able to secure part of the purchase money through a $75,000 loan from the Mennonites when Dr. John Smucker facilitated it through his relationship with the Mennonites. We had no signed contract, but we did have a verbal agreement to repay within ten years. My brother Rob's church also provided us with a partial start-up loan. Rob and I knew the great need for urban biblical and cultural training since most of the training was done out in the rural areas; thus, I proposed that Elim Bible Institute partner with us in this new faith endeavor. The leadership at Elim, however, chose not to partner with us, which was disappointing to me. Elim did agree, though, to send their students for urban training once the school got going. I thought my sixteen years of service at Elim was proof enough that would allow my brother, my Elim brethren, and me to step forward together in faith to build once again but, as it ended up, it was only my brother and me.

After years of waiting, Gloria and I made our way to relocate in New York City in July of 1984 to begin the New York School of Urban Ministry, otherwise known as NYSUM. Gloria had been very sick with polymyalgia rheumatica and was just beginning to feel better, so this would be a totally new venture for her. Further, just before we moved, her father passed away. To help us move, my brother sent his son Brian to Elim in a church van with a U-Haul trailer attached for us to pack all of our belongings into. Whatever belongings did not fit into the van and U-Haul, we left behind. We had moved so many times before, we knew it was best to go light and just add whatever we needed at the next location. We moved straight to New York City and into a tiny, two-room upstairs apartment next door to our new school building. I had asked some people who were already helping with NYSUM and who lived in the building next door if there were any apartments available nearby for us to rent. They told me there was a lady living nearby with an empty upstairs apartment, but she was not at all interested in renting it out. As soon as I heard that, I walked right out of the NYSUM building, knocked on her front door, and introduced myself as a fellow New Yorker. She invited me in for tea and Irish bread. We sat and chatted in her little kitchen. Soon she offered the apartment to Gloria and me, despite the fact that she had refused many others this opportunity. In order to access our new upstairs living quarters, we even had to walk through our landlady's apartment! The location, however, was perfect to be able to restore the new school building conveniently located right next door.

At this same time, Gloria and I were able to be a part of launching other church-related Bible schools besides the one at Brooklyn Tabernacle. Our dual vision of helping the local churches and building NYSUM was beginning to materialize. The NYSUM motto "A training and resource center serving the urban church" became a part of our culture and purpose.

Judy Ebersole and Rosemary Esch, who had already invested many hours of service praying, were sent to the City first and then we followed. Rosemary had a degree in culinary arts and was able to take care of the purchase of proper pots and pans, a stove, and everything else needed to cook for all of the students who would be enrolling. Judy Ebersole set up the student ministry scheduling, while Gloria exercised her bookkeeping skills once again for this brand new school. I became president, my brother was vice president, and Dr. John Smucker served as secretary/treasurer. We all became a part of the new teaching staff, and we were pleased to have Carlton Spencer, Elim's president emeritus, join our board. Once a week the staff gathered for a devotional time, and we shared in work time to make certain all who joined us knew the value of hard work. Without an army of volunteers, NYSUM could not have been raised up. Many churches and individuals offered long hours of hard work to see the building restored and the vision take shape. Most of the precious saints who went with us in this step of faith are still in the ministry today, albeit at various locations. None of us took any salaries for five years and very little salary after that.

The NYSUM motto:
"A training and resource center serving the urban church"

Our newly purchased school building conveniently had thirty-five bedrooms previously used as a residence for blind men. Wanting to give sight to the spiritually blind, straightway we faced the overwhelming challenge of transforming this ruined structure into a useful purpose once again. We moved forward seeing only one step at a time so as not to be overwhelmed. We kept in mind our vision to see the finished building as an all-in-one dormitory and urban training center as we repurposed this ruined place. We replaced all the doors that had been burned out; put in all new windows, a new roof, and a brand new oil boiler for heat; and got the plumbing working. As soon as it was made livable, we rented out ten of the thirty-five bedrooms to produce income to repay the mortgage and, praise God, we were able to pay our building loan from the Mennonites back in just seven years! Once we had the building paid off, we replaced the rented rooms with total ministry space. During the school year, we housed two students per room for a total of seventy students.

In the summers when the students went home, we kept the rooms full of people from all over who came to minister and to undergird the local church. We were always serving the local church. If a church wanted an outdoor meeting in the park or worship leading or puppet ministry or something else, we purchased everything needed to make it happen and sent a team to minister. Once we even bought an old truck and had a friend cut out the entire side of the truck to make a drop down "preaching platform." That old truck traveled all over the Big Apple providing positive preaching opportunities for students week after week. Many people accepted Christ by this means.

Those we sent to lead these meetings were trained to yield to the requesting pastor who was the one to lead people to a personal relationship with Jesus Christ and into a local church. These new believers could also access the feeding program we started serving through the local churches. Instead of directly handing out food ourselves, we flowed our ministry through and with the local churches so as to complement and not to compete with them. We made it our mission for the pastors to know that we were not there to overpower them or to usurp their authority. We were there only to help and to bless. In fact, in order to connect better with the local churches we even invited pastors in to share a meal and fellowship. We always made it our goal to focus on the manner or way we went about establishing NYSUM. We never told the people to come to NYSUM because that was the place God was moving, as if He weren't moving any other place. We made it clear that NYSUM was there to help the local churches. By going about establishing the school this way, our ministry is endeared to the New York City churches to this day. Rather than establishing a student-centered facility like many Bible schools, we founded a church-centered training center. We began training students from the start to assist the churches with a team mentality rather than an individualistic, me-centered mentality. This method produces a lot of growth and maturity in the students who are then able to flex with the changes. Working with the City's pastors is learning to plant one's feet in midair because things change all the time. The students are able to work with what is and not what is on any one person's personal agenda. Students' heads whirl around as plans change and their spirits hold firmly onto His Spirit. Concrete programs never trump necessary changes brought about by unforeseen circumstances. The schedules set between the NYSUM school and the many churches change still today, making the students' experiences more real world rather than cloistered. We held pastors' seminars, Christian workers' seminars, and Sunday school seminars well attended by churches throughout the City. For several years, we even hosted one-day pastors' wives seminars led by Gloria.

Another New York School of Urban Ministry related fruit that grew right away was complete Thanksgiving turkey dinners for local churches to distribute. In 1987 Peter and Darlene DeArruda enthusiastically joined us and continue there to this day. Peter and Darlene shared our vision and grafted securely into our team. Peter became a great instrument of preaching and leading students into street evangelism. Peter became executive vice president and eventually president of NYSUM.

In 1993 Peter DeArruda, my brother Rob, and I noticed nearby Boulevard Hospital sat empty. We were notified that the hospital building was to be auctioned off by its owner Johnson and Johnson of baby powder fame. In New Brunswick, New Jersey, we met and negotiated with the building's leaders who agreed to sell the building to us for 3 million dollars. Of course, we did not have any of the 3 million dollars at that time, but we knew God had the funding for anything and everything He wanted. When word got out that we were buying the old Boulevard Hospital, someone offered us 1.3 million dollars for the smaller, original building we were already using. It seemed like a good idea at first, but during a prayer meeting we were stopped by the Holy Spirit who directed us, "No. I have another way of doing it." Keeping the first smaller building a block away then, the board of which I was chairman decided to secure a mortgage. Rather than a bank mortgage, we obtained a 3.5 million dollar loan from the Assemblies of God. We refinanced in 2015 as a step on our way to our debt-free goal. Keeping the first, smaller building proved to be very wise because another way we work toward repaying our mortgage is by renting out space on the first floor to two doctors' groups. The groups' monthly rent pays not only the mortgage on the second building but also both buildings' operations. This income source has proven much steadier than a previous renter we had who went bankrupt, which caused the building to produce no income for a whole ten months. We had to go to bankruptcy court to force the renters to pay what had not been paid according to our signed contract. They ended up paying us $650,000. This was just one of many hassles we went through until we reached a steady spot where we could finally kick off our nine-month program (check out our website www.nysum.org for more info). Another income stream has produced on average over $10,000 a month income over the years from its use as a Christian dorm. In 2017 the original building was leased to another organization with a promise of substantial, long-range increased income.

By the grace of God, the ministry of New York School of Urban Ministry is still going strong today with the same motto as always: A training and resource center serving the urban church. We have people living there still, taking Bible-based courses, and strengthening the local churches. Beginning in 2016 our nine-month program called City Reach began with students enrolled for an in-depth nine month program. This is a part of the original vision, but because of many unforeseen obstacles we had to postpone certain things. However, as we continued strengthened in our faith and giving glory to God, we finally moved off the ground.

We so love all of the local churches and their pastors. Gloria and I are deeply grateful to all of the people who served to make NYSUM what it is today—a beacon of light to the City and the world.

After ten short years ministering among the churches of New York City and establishing the ministry of New York School of Urban Ministry, Gloria and I faced a crucial life decision once again. Was it time to linger longer or leave? A call to become president of Elim Bible Institute (later renamed Elim Bible Institute and College) came.

REFLECTION QUESTION:

When have you against all hope believed in God's promise to you?

CHAPTER 16

Final Roundabout to Elim

In 1994 I was informed Dr. Mike Webster, the president of Elim
Bible Institute, was going to step down from the position. I called
together key leaders to seek the Lord for two full days concerning
who would replace Mike. I needed to know how to keep the school
moving forward since I was chairman of the board at that time.
At the end of our two-day, concentrated prayer, all of the other
leaders concluded I was the one to fill the presidency. My initial
reaction was denial. I liked being in New York City. When I returned home I told Gloria what the other leaders had concluded
after prayer. Gloria's initial response was "I was afraid of that."

Wanting to know God's will for certain, Gloria and I went
on a personal retreat to the Pocono Mountains where we could
hear from God without interruption. While there, we read together the Bible story of the ark going back to Jerusalem as
recorded in 1 Samuel 6:7-12. As a test the Philistines placed the
ark on a cart and attached two milking cows that had been separated from their calves. If the cows left their calves and returned
to Jerusalem, they would know the plagues were from God. If
the cows would not leave their calves, then they knew what they
were experiencing was by chance. The cows did indeed leave
their calves and cross over into the ark's territory, but they did
so crying or "lowing all the way" (1 Sam. 6:12, NIV). Our assignment became clear and personal through this passage of
Scripture. Although this assignment was not what we really
wanted to do because we had already served at Elim sixteen
years prior, we wanted to obey God. When Gloria and I returned home from our prayer retreat in the Poconos, I called my
friend Reverend Tommy Reid who confirmed he already knew
I would become the president of Elim even before I shared with
him the news. Full Gospel Tabernacle, Orchard Park, New York,

with Pastor Reid was a dear support for the ten years we served at NYSUM before returning to Elim.

It was time to leave New York City. Elim Bible Institute needed a new president; I offered to serve in that position if the school's board had the same intention and desire. They happily accepted my offer, and Gloria and I tore ourselves away from NYSUM through many prayers and more tears because we were leaving our beloved home in the City. Feeling the support and approval from the Elim board and the student body, we moved back to Lima, New York, in August 1994.

What a fruitful time it was back at Elim! We saw growth in the student body in both numbers enrolled and depth of commitment to Jesus Christ working with our great team members. Traci Williams led the admissions department well, and I invited Jeff Clark who faithfully assisted me. When I arrived at Elim this time the enrollment was down to a total of less than 150 students. I spent the first year just observing what was happening on campus and noticing some bottlenecks to the flow. At the end of that year, I made some very careful changes. One of the changes I made was to move people from the wrong places into the right places for them. Another change I made was to place the sweet, young Lynda LaBarca into the position of fielding all of the admission inquiries and referring the calls to me for screening. Lynda researched the New York State laws concerning whether or not people could enroll at Elim before earning a high school equivalency diploma. She discovered that indeed a person could start at Elim and simultaneously earn a high school equivalency diploma. Lynda always remained positive and caring in her answers toward anyone who wanted to attend Elim.

Since the Holy Spirit never speaks more than necessary, I knew I should listen well when the Spirit spoke to me, "You are charging too much." Then I heard a specific number, "Five-thousand, eight-hundred, and fifty dollars." Directly, I asked Reverend David Edwards, president emeritus who had returned from Florida, to figure school costs up so the total would stay within the five-thousand, eight-hundred, and fifty dollar directive from above. The board agreed that if God had spoken, we would follow. Therefore, one of the first changes we made was to lower tuition costs by over $1000 a year as a way to increase enrollment. When the current student body heard we were lowering costs, they voiced their opinion that it was unfair since they had already paid a higher cost. After listening to their concerns, we decided to move ahead with the tuition cut we sensed was right, and the result the next year was nearly a 100 student enrollment increase! It was a total miracle. God had made it grow.

Our team oversaw more building projects in ten of my twelve year service than the school had seen in all of its existence. Our building projects included a brand new gymnasium, a student center with a dining hall, a twelve-unit married couples' apartment building, and a remodeling of the former Elim Fellowship office building into the library named after S. Joy Niswander. One person in particular really helped the fulfillment of the new dining hall; that person was Andy Spencer. Andy's father was one of the original partners who founded Elim Bible Institute, and Andy was a local farmer who continued his father's legacy by serving on the school's board of directors. Andy agreed that it was time to move forward into building an updated dining hall. Andy stated, "I believe we need to believe for 500." All the board members agreed that the new dining hall should hold 500 people at once in sharp contrast to the overcrowded, outdated cafeteria currently being used. Soon after, I was sitting at my desk when I prayed to know when to begin the construction. On that particular day I sensed that this was the day. I found a person on campus who had access to a shovel, so I asked him to go start digging a hole at a certain place on the ball field where we wanted the student center building located. The man with the shovel informed me he needed a blueprint in order to begin. I replied, "Not to dig a hole we don't!" And that was the humble way the campus student center got its start. From there we needed to have the soil tested at a cost of $2,300. That money came in a surprising way after we began to move forward. One day as I sat in my office, a former student I knew came in and handed me an envelope. He explained that his wife's father had died, leaving her a small inheritance. He further explained he and his wife wanted Elim to have some of that inheritance, and when I opened the envelope inside was $2,300! This was the seed money planted in good tested soil, resulting in a building filled with a modern kitchen, dining hall, dining room, rest rooms, offices, and all of the other "little" amenities that make the students feel at home in the Elim student center.

People from all around came to help build. Student Dale Stevens served as foreman, while I supervised the various building projects. Dale used students to do the manual labor, training them in the building trades at the same time. Dale's wife Lisa served as bookkeeper and Vard Gainor negotiated with the banks for the mortgage. Because we were building by faith, when we poured the cement for the basement of the campus center we rejoiced and held chapel on top of the new cement floor and under the open sky. Next, we completed building the succeeding floor, stopping long enough to hold chapel on that floor at its completion and rejoicing again. Finally, by the time the construction of the third and final floor came about, the New York winter was approaching with its shortened daylight hours, so we had to set up powerful lights inside to hold the chapel service there.

Once the metal frame was erected, Foreman Dale needed to find an experienced brick layer to lay the bricks. He heard about just such an expert by the name of Jim VanMaaren in the town of Lima, so he went to talk to this man who had not visited the campus for many years. Dale told him we needed to put brick on the outside of the building. Jim responded that he knew I was president of Elim, and that I used to be one of the teachers of the primary boys at Lima Baptist Church where he had attended as a pre-teen. This expert brick layer said I had taught him the Word of God, so he was willing now to come and do our brick-laying work. He brought his two sons to work with him, and we recruited enough other Elim students to do the work. He taught all of the students how to professionally lay brick. Many of these students later became bi-vocational pastor/brick layers using the brick laying skills they learned at Elim to earn a living while pastoring. We supplied everyone working with the materials they needed to keep the building moving forward in the same way Gramps had taught me early on. We moved step by step forward in faith; God provided for each step. Faith was built into the students by experiencing the believing and building process. At the end of one year of building, our expert brick layer charged us $43,000 for his and his sons' labor. That is all he charged us! It was a gift. Before long we were holding our final chapel and joyous celebration of our construction faith walk.

By the time all of our building projects were completed we did need to take out a mortgage, but in light of all we had saved and all we had built, the mortgage seemed small. All of this brought a new sense of progress and a renewed faith. Everyone watching saw we were obedient, and they witnessed He was faithful. It is not about money; it is about the obedience that comes from faith. The buildings immediately became filled with students both single and married, faith-filled graduates, special speakers like Dr. Pat Robertson of CBN who commented on the dramatic change he saw on campus since the last time he had visited, and valuable books donated by many, including the Elim Buffalo center. The name changed from Buffalo School of the Bible to Elim Buffalo during my tenure at Elim because of the combined leadership of Reverend Tommy Reid and me. Reverend Reid was the senior pastor of Full Gospel Tabernacle in Orchard Park, New York, when we worked together to bring the school located in his church building under Elim's covering. Hundreds of students, who possibly otherwise would not have had the opportunity to become well-trained ministers, were able to study and be trained through this merger and many of those graduates are still in the ministry today.

During my time at Elim, Pastor Mike Cavanaugh, the shepherd of Elim Gospel Church at that time, and I met on the Ivan Q. Spencer tabernacle platform on the Elim campus during a conference when Pastor Mike informed me Elim Gospel Church was looking to lease the tabernacle from Elim Bible Institute. But, standing there with the tabernacle packed full of people during that conference, we gave each other a knowing look—This tabernacle would not be big enough for what God wanted to do. Right then and there, we agreed the church needed its own new building. Soon the Elim school board decided to offer to give Elim Gospel Church ten acres of land the school owned so they could build in the center of the campus a building of their own. Under Mike's leadership then, Elim Gospel Church members did a beautiful job building their own new up-to-date church building instead of leasing the Elim tabernacle.

I also was able to direct improvements to the finishing touches on the Lima property, including having the school's small pond excavated and enlarged. After all of this building by faith—the student center, the library, the married student apartment, a gymnasium, and now a new church—the students themselves became inspired to raise the necessary funds to build the beautiful wooden Unity Bridge over the newly enlarged pond, connecting Elim Bible Institute to the new Elim Gospel Church. Faith begets faith.

One particular office visit stands out in my mind during this season at Elim because of the faith impact it created. It looked like it would be just another "ordinary" day in my president's office in 1996 when I was visited by Bishop Mophat Kilioba and his precious wife Donna. They had traveled from their home in Kenya to discuss the need they saw for PEFA to have a centrally located main office. As I listened carefully to their concern, I felt prompted to mention the Kenya Bible Society building located near All Nations Gospel Church's original warehouse in the city center of Nairobi. Unbeknownst to me, Donna was very familiar with the Bible Society building I had mentioned. She proceeded to inform me, "I work there and they want to sell it." Immediately, we joined in prayer because we knew we needed God's right hand and His holy arm to make such an impossibility possible. Next, PEFA's President Samuel Mwatha joined us, calling all of the PEFA-related churches together to raise the $340,000 price tag. Elim Fellowship decided to help by raising some of the funds needed for the building's down payment. We were in it together; however, the PEFA churches took the main responsibility for releasing this truly faith miracle purchase.

After twelve years of fruitful leadership at Elim, both Gloria and I sensed it was our time to retire from this great responsibility. Once again, we sensed the Holy Spirit leading us onward. This time we sensed, "Take . . . bread for your brothers . . ." straight from the Word of God. It happened when Gloria and I were reading one of the stories about David in I Samuel 17. The story goes something like this: Following his father's instructions to check on his brothers, David left his father's sheep in the care of a shepherd; loaded a wagon with grain, bread, and cheese; and headed for the front lines of battle. When I read out loud the five small words "Take . . . bread for your brothers" (v. 17), the words became alive to us. I said immediately to Gloria, "We are receiving our retirement assignment." (We never wanted to just wander around wondering what we were to do next.) Our questions in prayer then became Who are our brothers? and What is the bread? We needed clarity. We came to understand our brothers were all those people around the world we had been involved with and built relationships with over the years. They were our brothers and sisters who we knew in the Lord. Our next question followed: Where are the brothers? They are in the battle being stymied by a taunting giant who no one is challenging. I saw that God would send us to places where His people were struggling, being challenged as they encountered fear and resistance to moving forward. I knew we would be able to come alongside these people to bring a breakthrough by giving to them the necessary resources, healthy teachings, and a robust faith. It meant helping people we knew from Kenya; from Lima, New York; from New York City; from Mexico; Spain; China and a few other places. Although we are still asked to go many other places, we do not feel pressured to go because those new places do not fit with our specific assignment. We also came to understand the bread we were to take to our brethren was our possessions of provision, resources, teaching, and a spirit of faith. We were to come alongside and challenge our brethren to the battle, but we were never to leave them without the winning resources.

REFLECTION QUESTION:

Have you ever experienced a time when you tore yourself away from one place through many tears in order to obey God?

CHAPTER 17
Final Assignment

People define retirement in many ways; for me, Paul, it means "removing the hooks of responsibility while maintaining the concerns." The words from I Samuel 17 provided specific direction for both Gloria and me to transition into our new retirement assignment. The clock was ticking and the time had come for us to leave living at Elim in Lima, New York. We looked around for a suitable location to resettle before coming to the conclusion the best place to go would be Hampton, Virginia, where our son and his wife still live. Furthermore, Hampton is close to the Newport News and Norfolk airports making for easier travel for worldwide ministry out of our home base. No longer were we anchored at a particular location; we were anchored in God's directive to take bread to our brethren.

Leaving our responsibilities at Elim freed up my time enough to begin to write my first book entitled *Free by Divine Decree: Living Free of Guilt and Condemnation.* Our assignment to take resources to our brethren had begun. At this same right time, Elim alumna Jodi Hokenson became prepared and available to help with this book by taking the meticulously typed out Romans class notes and creating those notes into book form. In the initial printing, we were assisted by Reverend Bob Sorge whom we give thanks for because he agreed to print my first edition through his Oasis House publishing. Once the book was complete, I had 5000 copies printed in English, including an inspirational volume for new believers, and sold or distributed them to many hungry souls around the globe. Sensing the great need for the foundational principles found in this book that was born out of the materials I created for a class on Romans at Elim, we next had the book translated into Mandarin and in time distributed 45,000 copies in China; thirdly, we had the book translated into Spanish with the help of Andreas and Kelly Spyker of Mas Vida in Mexico and Elliot Tepper of Betel in Spain; and finally, we had the book translated and dedicated into Arabic in 2015 in Egypt. You might say it became a book for all peoples, tribes, tongues, and nations.

Continuing on with taking resources to our brethren, Dr. Brick Cliff and Nation-2-Nation (N2N) University helped me by video recording my teachings from Romans and distributing these recordings throughout the world in various languages. Nation-2-Nation has produced many important teachings by experienced pastors, doctors, and leaders. My Romans teachings developed into a series of twelve 35-minute lessons complete with a very detailed study guide. N2N also produced my Acts and Hebrews teachings into sets of twelve, 35-minute courses and my Biblical Ethics course into a set of ten lessons, each one with detailed written study guides. All of these writings and teachings are available through pauljohansson@gmail.com or *www.winministries.org*. These courses together represent my life message, and I rejoice today knowing these teachings are in many languages and will, Lord willing, be translated into many more as a way of building solid, strong Christians around the globe.

During our "retirement" many doors opened keeping in line with our specific assignment to take bread to our brethren. One such open door has been in Mexico where Elim graduates John and Marla Spyker and their Elim graduate son Andreas and daughter-in-law Kelly Spyker serve. Their work has grown healthily. About thirty years ago John Spyker invited me to join him on the western coast of Mexico at a coastal city called Lazaro Cardenas. He and his wife had founded a small church there. We flew into Mexico City and after our plan to travel by air from that city to Lazaro Cardenas fell through, we were forced to take the thirteen-hour bus ride around hairpin mountain turns sitting in a loosely secured bus seat. As I sat uncomfortably dozing off, I had a vision of a wave coming out of the Pacific Ocean, traveling up the mountain and right over the bus I was in, and moving all the way on to Mexico City. I saw that when the wave receded, there were pools of water left throughout the mountains. I understood the Lord was letting me know that what He was doing was going to be a celebration of worship beginning in the lowly places down on the coast and ending in Mexico City. As it stands today there are 166 churches in the mountains where I had seen pools of water after the wave covered the mountains in my vision. One place the worship wave arrived was in Morelia, where John's son Andreas later became pastor. That church now runs between 5000 and 6000 people. In early 2015 the Spykers informed me that they had not fulfilled the initial vision because the worship revival from the coast had not made it to Mexico City yet. In just over the next six months, the church in Morelia raised over $100,000 to set up a meeting place in Mexico City. There were 2000 people in the first service including Gloria and me. The church soon moved from its first location to a more reasonably priced building with a thousand-person capacity. After just six months the church was able to hold almost a thousand people every Sunday. The Morelia church decided to create a three minute video showing the wave in my vision, which electrified the audience to launch out. Andreas and Kelly moved with the wave right into Mexico City where they continue to see growth.

Another open door for us is in Nairobi, Kenya. I fly back and forth giving direction to the elders as I am invited. They always warmly receive me, take great care of me, and pay my in-country expenses, never asking me for any finances. They are always giving. We did not plant the seed of entitlement or dependency those many years ago; we planted the seed of life, which is yielding its good and multiplied fruit.

A third door to our brethren continues in New York City through NYSUM and a fourth open door is through the drug rehab program named *Betel*, which began in the slums of Madrid, Spain, and has expanded most recently into India. I have gladly served on *Betel's* board of directors for many years. Fellow Elim graduates Elliot and Mary Tepper moved to Spain from Mexico. At first Elliot attempted to evangelize using the old, traditional key he had used in Mexico; however, he quickly learned that each city has its own, unique key and going door-to-door was not the right key to Madrid. So, he went out to the hurting in Canblas. When he saw the desperate, hurting people, he and his wife Mary decided to bring a couple of them into their home to live with them and their three sons. Now these hurting people started out stoned out of their minds with all of the accompanying problems dragging along, but this small act of kindness has grown into a multitude of self-supporting outreach centers in fifty nations of the world. When Mary passed away a few years ago, her United States' funeral was held in Wilmington, North Carolina. The first couple from Spain who had worked through the *Betel* way of life in the Tepper's home attended. They spoke the following words at Mary's funeral while retelling the story of when Elliot and Mary took them into their home: "Eliot and Mary were trusting us when we did not trust ourselves."

Two-thousand and fifteen was a full traveling year; I spent a few weeks in Asia (God alone knows of our brethren in Asia to whom we have been able to take bread) where I reunited with Kevin Graves, one of my former Elim students. Kevin went from Elim to New York School of Urban Ministry and on to Asia. I no sooner returned home when I flew off to Egypt with Pastors Ron and Judy Burgio; returned home when Gloria and I flew to Mexico; returned home; and our son Mark and I flew to India and Kenya, touching base with all of our brethren on the front lines before landing back home just in time for Christmas.

One of the responsibilities I have stepped away from while continuing to carry the concern includes my thirty-three year commitment to Blue Mountain Christian Retreat in New Ringgold, Pennsylvania. For all those years I served as the keynote speaker at their amazing urban men's retreat, a multi-ethnic gathering of more than 500 men, and as an annual speaker at their Memorial Day conference. A second responsibility I have removed myself from is my ten year commitment of serving as chairman of the board of directors for the Great Commission Coalition. This coalition began when Elim graduates Tom and

Mercy Victor desired to bring believers together for prayer and continues through their leadership of gathering people for a prayer focus in the United States and connecting to prayer groups in developing nations. Thirdly, I have stepped away from serving on the board of Christ Church in Montclair, New Jersey, with Pastor David Ireland. Fourthly, I stepped down from forty years of serving as one of the council of elders at Elim Fellowship, which oversees many churches and international workers. Other capable leaders are able to take my former places of responsibility while I continue to care deeply about these ministries.

With our new freedom from our former hooks of responsibility, our hearts sing a new song because we are able to encourage and love more deliberately on our children Marcia and Mark; grandchildren Andrew, Katie, Paul and Ryan and their spouses; plus all of our beautiful great-grandchildren. We are in a greater position not only to rejoice with our family, but also to "mourn with those who mourn" (Rom. 12:15b). Gloria and I have shared deeply in the family grief from the loss of both sets of our parents, and most recently the sudden loss of my twin brother, Rob, who passed into eternity in October of 2016 and who was such a vital part of our life and ministry.

Gloria and I together also rejoice reflecting on over sixty years of a fruitful marriage and ministry for God. But, the end of our story is not finished yet; we continue to fight the giants of unbelief wherever God sends us. In the words of my favorite poem "I Stand by the Door" written by Reverend Sam Shoemaker: "So I shall stand by the door and wait, For those who seek it." I took Reverend Shoemaker's entire poem as my philosophy of ministry and life. The following is an excerpt from that poem that has imparted more life to me than words can convey:

> I stand by the door.
> I neither go too far in, nor stay too far out,
> The door is the most important door in the world—
> It is the door through which people walk
> when they find God.

I urge everyone to read and ponder the entire poem over and over again.

REFLECTION QUESTION:

Who has helped you accomplish your God-given assignments?

CHAPTER 18
Looking Forward

Now that we have both celebrated over eighty years of abundant living, there will never be a day when Gloria and I leave behind the love we feel for all of the beautiful people we have come across. It is as if a strong cord of love has entwined us for eternity. However, our bodies cannot possibly keep up the pace we once did being fully committed and involved in whatever assignments our Lord and Savior brought to us at home and abroad. Going forward we know our place is on the sidelines coaching and cheering the team on to certain victory, while occasionally sending in new plays to fresh, young "quarterbacks." The experiences we have gained over the years, we are still using to teach, encourage, consult, and root on God's overcoming team of pastors and leaders. In all of our life and ministry we proclaim "not ourselves, but Jesus Christ as Lord" (2 Cor. 4:5a, NIV) because "we have this treasure in jars of clay to show that this all-surpassing power is from God and not from us" (v. 7). We have been, are, and will be His instruments on His assignments who, because we believe we speak, since "we have that same spirit of faith" (v. 13) that powerfully "raised the Lord Jesus from the dead" (v. 14).

It is high time for the next generation of believers to take their turn, to look for their faith assignments, and to allow God to write their stories. As the giants of unbelief are shown defeated, this next generation is preparing for victory! "Now faith is the substance of things hoped for, the evidence of things not seen" (Heb. 11:1, NKJV). Failure is impossible. The church with all of its differences remains faithfully united around the cross of Jesus Christ; He is the object of our faith and His cross is and always will be the center of full, ultimate victory! Amen.

REFLECTION QUESTION:

*What loving assignment has God given you
for such a time as this?*

Spencer Hall Administrative
Building at Elim

The house we built in Lima

Mark & Mary
wed 1977

First NYSUM
Board: John Smucker,
Robert Johansson,
Carlton Spencer,
Paul Johansson

First building:
46th Street

NYSUM Building

Paul & Gloria in front of NYSUM

Peter & Darlene DeArruda

The Johansson Clan

Our 48th Street house in NY

Installation as EBI President

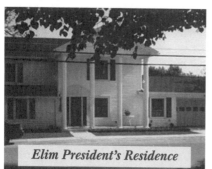

Elim President's Residence

EBI Student Center

Five Elim Presidents: Carlton Spencer, David Edwards, Michael Webster, Paul Johansson, Jeffrey Clark

Mark's Graduation from SUNY Geneseo

Marcia's Graduation, MA University of Rochester, 1999

Mark and Family

Two sets of twins: Paul & Ryan Herlan; Paul & Rob Johansson

Marcia's Doctorate Graduation

Our house in Hampton, Virginia

Free by Divine Decree

Paul, Indian leader, Elliot Tepper and Mark Johansson

Delhi Conference with Betel Ministry

Betel Church in Spain

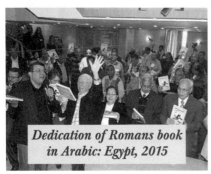

Dedication of Romans book in Arabic: Egypt, 2015

Paul preaching in Mombasa church, Kenya

Morelia, Mexico; Mas Vida Church; Andreas & Kelly Spyker

Dedication of Romans book in Mandarin

Mark & Mary Johansson

Paul & Gloria

Andrew, Emily, Caleb, Hazel and Levi Johansson

Marcia & John Marquardt

Peter, Katie, Eleanor and Lillian Stern

Paul, Keri and Lana Herlan

Ryan, Jenn and Renley Herlan